D1440038

THE SOLWAY PLAINSMEN

LIFE'S QUALITY FOR THE CUMBRIAN HUNTINGTONS FROM THE 12TH TO THE 20TH CENTURY.

BY DOUGLAS HUNTINGTON

PUBLISHED BY : HELMWIND BOOKS.

The Solway Plainsmen

First published in Great Britain in 1995.

by Helmwind Books

an imprint of Crawley Industrial Press Limited
of Units 3-7, The Bell Centre,
Newton Road, Crawley, West Sussex, RH10 2FZ

Printed and bound in Great Britain by
Crawley Industrial Press Limited, The Bell Centre, Newton Road Crawley,
West Sussex RH10 2FZ.

British Library Cataloguing in Publication Data
is available from the British Library.

ISBN 0 9525941 0 2

CONTENTS

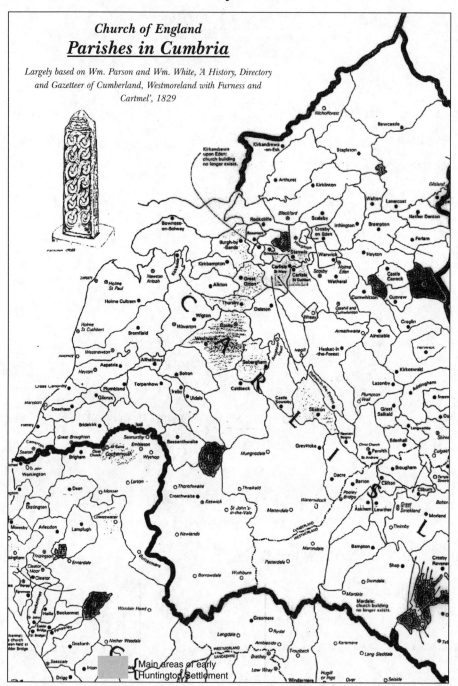

Church of England
Parishes in Cumbria

Largely based on Wm. Parson and Wm. White, 'A History, Directory and Gazetteer of Cumberland, Westmoreland with Furness and Cartmel', 1829

ILLUSTRATIONS

ALL MAPS BY COURTESY OF CUMBRIA ARCHIVES

Preface by the Author

Many times my wife June has commented how much she would love to warp back in time, to see how people really lived, "just for a few hours, mind you".

My reply has usually been to the effect that I thought experience of the smell, alone, would cause her to regret having made that wish, but if not, then her exposure to all sorts of diseases might render her return ticket superfluous in a short time.

That is easily said, but in truth our understanding of the real conditions which our ancestors, of not so long ago, endured, is quite meagre, because there is little in our current experience with which to make comparisons.

Therefore, having decided in the first instance, to trace my forbears, of whom I knew very little, I realised, that done, that I merely had a list of names and dates, with no knowledge of their way of life. To correct that shortcoming, I set about reading everything on which I could lay my hands, to tell me about Cumbria, and about the people who had lived there over the centuries. Numerous people and organisations went to quite extra- ordinary lengths to help me, by recommending books and documents to read, or to locate and obtain them for me. My nearest public lending library is at East Grinstead, in West Sussex, and they really did enter into the spirit with enthusiasm, by meeting the challenge of my demands - with a smile.

Having read all that time allowed me, and put the results to paper, I realised how inadequate had been my attempts at description, of living conditions; how poorly I had explained the causes of the numerous sad and early deaths which I had recorded. It had come as a shock to me, when, during my researches of the family of Huntingtons who lived at Skelton as recently as 1840, that it had been almost completely wiped out within the space of a few years; not completely, otherwise I should not be here, but very nearly. How could it happen that in such a pretty little village bordering on the fertile Eden Valley eleven Huntingtons were living in 1840, and that within a few years, only three survived? Two of these survivors were my great- grandfather, who had been born in 1836, and his young brother Joseph, who had been born in 1839, and these were cared for successively by their relatives, until these also succumbed, and later by kind family friends, such as the Grindals.

The culprits of these epidemic deaths were usually under-nourishment, and appalling sanitation. In the case of Skelton, it is difficult to conceive that these country people could have suffered from lack of food; after all, have you or I ever seen a hungry farmer? But then, it is necessary to recall that those times were referred to as the 'hungry forties'. The Corn Laws, until they were repealed in the mid-forties, caused havoc to food production, and it was the poor people who bore the brunt of the result.

Bad sanitation is something which we tend to associate with urban life; we feel that the countryman is spared its dangers.

This is untrue. Water was drawn from wells or water courses which were polluted by human and animal sewage, and it took the few people who had an inkling of the dangers, a long time to persuade the authorities of the dire need to educate the public about sanitation, and to provide facilities for its improvement.

I was recently reading a newly published biography, of theBronte family, was written by Dr.Juliet R.V.Barker, whose lives spanned this very same period, and spent in the Yorkshire village of Haworth - not so very far from Cumbria. I was struck by a passage in this book which described the standard of sanitation in Haworth; so descriptive was it that it that the smell it evoked nearly blew my hat off, and with permission from the author, and the publishers, Weidenfeld & Nicolson, I quote some of it below:

"Three-quarters of the way up Main Street is Lodge Street, which is as all alleys and sidestreets in Haworth used to be: a narrow dirt track, six to eight feet wide, with a pavement of stone flags to keep the pedestrian out of the muck. As late as 1850, there were still no sewers and few covered drains; the surface water, combined with household waste, and what a report into the sanitation of Haworth politely called the 'effluvium' of privies and midden-steads, ran along open channels and gutters down the streets.."

"Ill health was exacerbated by the poor quality of the water supply. By 1850 there were eleven pumps, only nine of which were in use, and seven wells (one belonging to the parsonage), of which only two were public. One hundred and fifty inhabitants were dependent on the supply from Head Well which in summer ran so slowly that the poor had to start queuing there at two or three o'clock in the morning in order to get their water for their Monday wash; sometimes it ran so green and putrid that even the cattle refused to drink it. The water was tainted by the overflow from the midden-steads, which every house with access to a backyard seems to have possessed. These were walled enclosures into which all the solid household waste was thrown, including offal, ashes and the refuse of the privies. Every now and again, the local farmers would come round and take away the contents to spread on the fields, but sometimes the tips were overflowing, as in the case of the druggist's house, where the midden-stead was actually against the back wall of the house, and was piled up to the height of the larder window. There was not a single water closet in the whole of Haworth, and only sixty nine privies: some two dozen houses, including the parsonage, had their own (privy), but most households had to share, and there were at least two instances where twenty-four households were sharing a single privy. The 1850 Report notes that

Two of the privies, used by a dozen families each, are in the public street, not only within view of the houses, but exposed to the view of passers-by.........................

It was no surprise to the Inspector to find that the mortality rates in Haworth rivalled those in the worst districts in London: in Haworth, as Patrick (Bronte) was soon to discover, over forty- one per cent of children died before reaching their sixth birthday"

DOUGLAS HUNTINGTON, BONAVENTURE, MAY 1995.

Acknowledgments

To the staff at the Archives Office of the Cumbria Council, and most especially to Mrs Anne Howells, who gave, in addition to her time, much constructive advice and encouragement, during the research. Her colleagues, Lynda Collin, Vivienne Gate, and "The Boss", Jim Grisenthwaite, likewise gave generously of their help. Having consulted quite a few Record Offices in the course of researches, I believe that Carlisle beats them all for its dedication to help.

Thanks also to the staff of South London College for the help they rendered in connection with William Huntington; best wishes to them, they celebrate the centenary this year, of their re- location to new premises in South Norwood, London, in 1895, when William Huntington became their first Director.

So many people have entered into the spirit of helping with my research, for which I am extremely grateful, but I must mention the following: Mrs Winnie Bell, of Mawbray, herself a keen family historian, a Jefferson by birth, who, though in her late 70s, kindly went out and photographed Bog Farm for me, and later guided me on an exploration of the country surrounding Abbeytown: Mrs Dorothy Wannop, of Dalston, a newly found sixth cousin, who, with, I think, her daughter's assistance, pointed me in the direction to contact several other sixth cousins; likewise to Mrs Anne Willis (nee Huntington), the War Bride in reverse, who among other achievements, gave us cricketer Bob Willis; to Mrs Lyn Harpham, of Tauranga, New Zealand, and Professor Paul Phillips, of Tennessee University, yet another sixth cousin; to Margaret Willis, (so far as I know, no relation) of Thursby, who kindly provided some photographs of that village; to Captain John Huntington, who represents the only member of the families depicted in the chapter on Cockermouth, whom I have come across, and who provided a wealth of information and material; we must be related, but our common ancestry must be buried way back in pre- Elizabethan times; lastly to Heather Herbert, of Port Carlisle, to Frank and Eileen Pearson who kindly took photographs in the Sebergham area, to Mr Wilson Swan who also took some splendid photographs for me; and lastly to Mr Graham Morley, Headmaster of the school at Skelton, who also took some photographs.

Many much closer relatives have helped in the research by providing information, especially big-brothers Gordon Huntington, who came up with several treasures, and Ken Huntington; cousins Audrey Malby, Pamela Turner-Smith in South Africa, and Ian Huntington, in New Zealand; second cousin, Robert Simonds, who has got the Simonds family well documented, has given much encouragement; to younger son Guy Huntington, who started it all by asking questions which I was not able to answer at the time; to my son Warwick, for his generous contribution in printing this book; and to my wife June, who has patiently endured living with a pre-occupied mind for over three years, and who has nonetheless entered into the spirit of enthusiasm necessary to pursue this project.

Last of all, thanks to the voluntary librarians, Joe and Jean Hinge, at the library of the Crawley Mormon Church, whose help I enjoyed for three years of research.

John Huntington

APOTHECARY
Admitted a Freeman of
the Carlisle Merchants
Guild on Low Sunday
Quarter day Ap·26·1717

LIST OF FAMILY TREES.

NOTES:

THOSE NAMED IN THE FOLLOWING CHARTS ALL DESCENDFROM THE
FAMILIES DEPICTED IN CHART NO.2, WITH THEIR ORIGINS IN THE
WIGTON, WESTWARD, THURSBY AREA : 3,4,5,6,7,8,9,10,11,12,13,14,15,16,20, AND
21 (WHICH INDICATES THE ANCESTORS OF MARTHA)
THOSE NAMED IN THE FOLLOWING CHARTS ALL DESCEND FROM PERSONS
NAMED IN CHART NO.6 : CHART NOS. 7,8,9,10,11,12,13,14,15,16 AND 21,
NAMELY THEY ARE ALL DESCENDANTS OF JOHN & MARTHA.
THIS LEAVES THE QUAKERS IN CHART NO.1, AND THE COCKERMOUTH
BRANCHES. IT IS BELIEVED THAT THE COCKERMOUTH BRANCH WAS
LINKED TO THE QUAKERS, WHO INITIALLY CAME FROM BURGH-BY-SANDS.
THEY HAD LEFT THE ESTABLISHED CHURCH IN 1655. POSSIBLY, AT ABOUT
THAT TIME, SOME OF THEIR FAMILY RE-SETTLED IN THE COCKERMOUTH
AREA, AND IT MUST BE REMEMBERED THAT ANOTHER POPULAR MEETING
PLACE FOR QUAKERS WAS PARDSHAW, NEAR COCKERMOUTH. THIS HOW-
EVER MUST BE REGARDED AS SPECULATION.

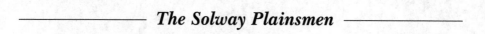

Dedication

I DEDICATE THIS BOOK TO MY WIFE, JUNE,
AND THE PROFITS, IF ANY, FROM THIS EDITION,
TO THE EDEN VALLEY HOSPICE.

CHAPTER ONE

SETTLERS IN CUMBERLAND

"Although we know so much about
Kings and statesmen, about the growth
of Parliament, and the rise of the
British Empire, we know very little
about the life of the average man and
woman in early modern England.
Indeed, we do not know whether all
our ancestors had enough to eat."
(Peter Laslett, in" The world we have lost"1965.)

"The world we have lost is lost forever -
but perhaps we shall begin to understand
what it once was."
(Andrew B.Appleby, in "Famine in Tudor and Stuart England", 1978)

At the time of the Norman Conquest, Malcolm, the son of the murdered Macbeth, (or possibly the son of that Malcolm, also named Malcolm) reigned over Scotland, of which Strathclyde was a part, and in turn of which Cumbria, at Malcolm's accession, was a part.

These were turbulent times, however, and in about 1070, Gospatric, Earl of Northumberland, over-ran the 'District of Caerlluel', in other words, Cumbria, in reprisal for the devastation of Teesdale by the Scots. Gospatric put his son Dolphin in charge of the territory.

The Normans, having presumably spent a quarter of a century after their conquest of England digesting its fruits, turned their attention to the north, and "In the year 1092", the Anglo-Saxon Chronicle tells us, "The King William (Rufus), with mickle fyrd, went north to Carlisle, and the borough set up again, and the castle reared, and Dolphin outdrove that ere the land wielded; and the castle with his men set, and sith hither south went, and mickle many of churlish folk with wives and cattle thither sent to dwell in the land to till it."

In modern language:" In this year, King William went north to Carlisle with great levies, and restored the town, and built the castle. He drove out Dolphin who had formerly ruled that district and garrisoned the castle with his men. Thereafter he returned hither southwards, sending very many peasants thither with their wives and cattle, to settle there, and to till the soil."

Later, the historian, Mr.Edward A. Freeman put it in a concise manner: "The unbroken English life of Carlisle begins with the coming of the Red King, and the settlement of his colony", and "The Red King not only called Carlleul into a new existence, but he planted in its district a Saxon Colony from the south, and thus superimposed on the previous elements a new ethnological graft". With his concise eloquence, Mr.Freeman continued: "For at least two hundred years before William came, it had been British or nothing. For at least two hundred years before that, it had been part of an English Kingdom, that of the Angles of Northumbria. For at least two hundred years before that, it had shared the

1

independence of those parts of Britain from which the Romans had gone, and into which the Angle or Saxon, had not yet come."

There are strong circumstantial grounds for believing that a family of Huntingtons was among those transplanted from the south, at the behest of the Red King, around the beginning of the twelfth century. The name Huntington is without doubt an Anglo- Saxon one, and in tracing its incidence in Cumberland, this seems originally to have been concentrated on the Solway Plain, and the indications are that the early families lived in the Thursby/Burgh by Sands area, and only as they multiplied did they spread further afield on the Plain.

The earliest mention of the presence of Huntingtons in Cumberland is to be found in the International Genealogical Index, 1992, as follows:

" HUNTINGTON, ADA, BIRTH ABOUT 1150 "

" HUNTINGTON, MAUD, BIRTH ABOUT 1152 "

Enquiries of the compilers and publishers of the International Genealogical Index, The Church of Jesus Christ of the Latter Day Saints, (The Mormons), elicits that one of their members, the late Hal.W.Sherman, had apparently discovered their connection with his ancestry, and in 1934, in keeping with Mormon practice, had prompted a 'baptism of the Dead'.

Claire Dyreng, proxy....inst. Hal W Sherman.
   40809 All of England.
Agatha of Normandy, b. about 1070, d. unknown, rel.
   40810
Adela (Alice) de Normandy, of England, d.1137 relative
   40811
 de Vermondois, Isobel, of Surrey Co. England, d.1131 relative
   40812
 de Northumberland, Sybil, of Northumberland Co. Eng. d.1040 26-cousin
40813
Margaret of Scotland, b.abt.1035, Scotland, d.unknown 26 cousin
   40814
Mary of Scotland, b.abt.1080, of Scotland, d.unknown 26 cousin
   40815
Waltheof, Maud, b.abt. 1090, of Northumberland, Co. Eng.
                     d.unknown, 24-g-g-son
                     All of Cumberland Co. Eng.
   40816
Huntingdon, Ada, b.abt.1150, d.unknown, rel.
   40817
Huntingdon, Maud, b.abt.1152, d.unknown,relative.

It has so far been impossible to discover the sources for the research which enabled Mr.Sherman to identify an ancestral connection with those listed above; neither is it very important for the purposes of the author's exercise, which is to indicate the strong likelihood of the existence of a pair of Huntingtons in Cumberland as early as the twelfth century.

The fact that the Huntingtons seem to have been settled initially on the Solway Plain, close to the Firth, also adds some credence to this belief, because there is little doubt that King William's purpose was not only to people the district with some loyal elements, but also to beef up the guarding of the borders against the depredations of the Scots. This required potential defenders to be positioned all along the Solway coast, for it was possible for marauders to cross the firth as far west of Bowness, and for raiders by boat to attack even further west. For this purpose these 'militia' were allowed tenancies of land for cultivation on favourable terms, often being exempted from taxes in return for border service. Similarly their security of tenure was often better than that of many tenants.

The area in which they lived however, suffered much turbulence for two or three centuries, being frequently the battlefield over which the English and the Scots fought for possession of Cumbria. Indeed, not until the end of Queen Elizabeth the First's reign at the beginning of the seventeenth century, did comparative peace prevail, with the union of the two crowns.

No records exist, which tell us anything about the lives of the Huntingtons in Cumberland, between their initial settlement in that County, and the late 16th century. The earliest documentary mention found is dated 1564; the inventory to the will of William Threlkeld, Bailiff of Burgh by Sand includes provision for a debt of sixteen shillings to 'Adem Huntington and John Lawson for thare haye'.

Another will, dated 1588, by Edward Threlkeld,' Clerk, Doctor of the Lawe, and Canon Resident in the Cathedral Church of Hereford, left a number of bequests to relatives, and to retainers also, including some to 'Rinian Huntington thirtene poundes six shillings eighte pence, (in today's money about £700) and my best trottinge geldinge, or ells insted of the geldinge, six poundes thirtene shillings fower pence at his choise. Also I doe give and bequeathe to the saide Rinian Huntington my twoe leases, viz. the one is of my garden beyonde the Castle Mills which I howlde by lease of Roger Cumberlache and his sonnes for yeares yett enduringe, and thother lease is of the demise or graunte of the Custos and vicars chorall of the Cathedrall Church of Hereford of a certeyne barn lyinge in the Barshamstrete now in myne owne occupation.'

****

These wills, however, apart from signalling to us that the family by then, was well absorbed into communities in Cumberland, tell us nothing about how, in the preceding four centuries, the Huntingtons settled in and survived.

It is likely that they began, at the end of the eleventh century, very near to the bottom of the pile; possibly the requirement to migrate was stipulated as an alternative to more severe punishment for crimes committed, rather in the same way that, in later times, criminals were given the option of penal or capital, punishment or of migrating, as virtual slaves, to the American colonies. This though, is thought unlikely. The need was for loyal and hardworking citizens to settle in the newly recovered lands. It is more likely, therefore, that the peasants were induced to migrate with the promise of allocations of land on newly created manors.

Let us imagine then, for imagine we must, without any records to help, that, at the beginning of the twelfth century, William Huntington, and his younger brother, Henry, the only children of Joseph and Mary Huntington to survive the hardships of the long journey from the south, and of struggling to establish themselves in their new environment, were helping their father on his twenty acres of land, at Boustead, near to the village of Burgh.

The help they gave at this time in their early lives was somewhat sporadic, for the land which the family tilled was close to the ancient Roman Wall, which stretched out of sight , in both directions, to the east and west. Although the wall was crumbling in many parts from depredations by both weather and thieving villagers, it offered great sport to children. Armed with crude, make- believe swords and spears, they could pretend they were adult defenders against the raiders from across the Solway, or, together with other children from the village, they could mount imaginary raids themselves between parties of them, divided into attackers and defenders. The attackers would rise out of the marshy grasses which stretched, at that point, from the remains of the wall to the edge of the sea, and charge noisily, with brandished weapons, at a vulnerable point. Here the defenders at the wall would assail them with clods of soil until hand to hand defence was possible.

During this time, Joseph and Mary, along with the other parents tilling their land, would keep a careful eye on their youngsters, to make sure that the skirmishing did not get too rough, or that the clambering about the walls did not become too risky. Apart from this they did not mind too much the games which the children played, for like kittens at play, the make-believe fighting did serve a purpose of eventually fitting them for skills which might one day preserve their lives from real attacks.

For although a large stretch of water separated these villagers from their unfriendly counterparts on the other side of the Solway Firth, the safety which this offered from attack, could quickly prove illusory; usually, but not exclusively, at night when darkness shielded raiders from view until they were ashore in their small boats. The villagers knew also, that boats were not essential for would-be raiders to make a crossing, and they were constantly being reminded that, as far west, to their left, as Bowness it was possible for men with knowledge of the estuary, to make their way across on foot, when the tide was low.

They knew also, that the Roman Wall, designed and built as it had been, to be manned strongly by bodies of well trained, and well armed soldiers, was no protection for them, part-time militia as they were. Rather they viewed the wall as a source of stone for them to filch, as useful material with which to strengthen their simple cottages. Constructed as they were from clay and rubble, these homes did not last long, and the stones from the wall were welcome, being ready to hand. This practice, however, was not encouraged by the Lord of the Manor, Ranulph de Meschin, who, although his seat was in faraway Appleby, employed a vigorous and strict Steward to look after his holdings on the plain. A blind eye might be turned from minor pilfering as long as it remained in that category; after all the Steward himself was not above having some building material dragged to his own tenement from time to time.

Joseph and Mary Huntington had lived at Burgh for nearly eight years, following their long, nightmare journey from the fenlands of Lincolnshire. They had not been sorry to uproot themselves from that region, because it had remained a lawless part long after the Norman Conquest. It had always been so, long before the Normans came, and after their coming, its comparative inaccessability had made pacification by the newcomers difficult. Whilst Joseph had not taken any part in the rebellious behaviour of his fellow Anglo-Saxons; (after all, as a landless peasant before their arrival, he had not been a loser by their coming), he longed to get away from a part where all inhabitants, rebellious or not, were constantly under suspicion.

They had not, however, counted on the terrible nature of the journey north, nor of the stark primitiveness of the conditions which they had to endure for the first year or so of their life on the Solway Plain. The journey had grievously caused the deaths of two of their children, who it seemed had succumbed through exhaustion, and three months after their arrival, their eldest son, John had died. This was a terrible blow, particularly as John, within a few more years would have been valuable help with the arduous job of land clearance, and cultivation. So Joseph and Mary had to face this task on their own, and to wait until first William and then Henry were old enough to provide more than light duties for the household. As soon as John had died, Joseph and Mary realised that her active help on the land could be interrupted by further pregnancies, and that there was only one sure way to prevent these - total abstinence. Their exhaustion at the end of each day's work aided them in this resolve.

Now, after a few years, having cleared enough of their twenty acres to provide sufficient food, their lives were becoming a little more bearable, though unfortunately quite a lot of their ground , sloping down towards the wall, was peat and moss, and never would be very productive. Joseph had decided that he would apply to the Lord of the Manor for some more land in due course. But he would wait until he was cultivating, to the maximum, the arable parts of the land he already held. His sons too, in a couple of years, would be able to make a bigger contribution to the work of husbanding his holding, and he felt that his plea would fall on more sympathetic ears when that situation prevailed.

****

William, now twenty years old, was ploughing his land to be ready for the spring sowing, when his mother, Mary came running across the field, obviously in some distress. He prayed to himself that she wouldn't be carrying the news which he feared most of all. It was nearly five years now since the Big Raid,in which the Scots, in addition to destroying many of the village cottages, and stealing much livestock, mainly sheep and pigs, had carried off into slavery William's brother, Henry. Henry would be seventeen now, and although the condition of many of their neighbours in Burgh was equivalent to serfdom, this was nowhere as dreadful as being helplessly at the mercy as well as at the beck of savage Scots across the water. William still missed his brother grievously, and their loss of yet another child had proved an unbearable blow to Joseph and Mary; most especially to Joseph, for, as so often is the case, the mother proved to be the more resilient. The spirit seemed to have been knocked out of Joseph; no more did he talk of claiming a bigger piece of land, and increasingly he had tended of late to leave more of the work and responsibility to his remaining son, William.

Now, as his mother came nearer he could see that she was in tears, and he did not wait to drop the plough; he ran towards her and the cottage. His worst fears were borne out; his father had collapsed and died in Mary's arms, and he stood at the threshold, realising that he was the head of the household, and now totally responsible.

It was his good fortune that it was the custom of the manor that, he being the inheritor of his father's tenancy, along with his mother, was not called upon to pay the heriot on the occasion of his father's death, nor the fine required on the transfer of the tenancy. This was because the terms of this borderland tenancy excused him from these taxes, in return for his assuming the obligations of liability for militia duty. Fortunately he was a strong young man, and equally fortunately Mary, his mother remained a fit and strong woman, though she was fifty-five years old.

William was a hard worker; he had long put behind him the days of puppy-like play among the ruins of the wall; he had also put away his earlier dreams of crossing to Scotland to find and rescue his brother Henry; his first duty was to care for and protect his mother, for he realised that, without him, she would soon lose the land, and would become a pauper; besides, Henry was better able to take care of his own survival than was his mother.

Because he was a hard worker, always did more than his share of the Boon work,and undertook the 'night-watch', and, militia duties conscientiously, William was popular with the villagers of Burgh, and also with the Steward of the manor, Rowland Finlinson. The latter also came from peasant stock; his father had been one of the migrants to arrive a few years before William's father, and he admired the way in which, despite his youth, William had assumed his responsibilities.

When therefore William petitioned at a Court Leet, for permission to marry Jannet Pattinson, a daughter of another villager, the Steward recommended his Lord's approval, which was duly granted, subject to the customary fine to be paid by Jannet's father. This, the father did not mind paying, as he would thereafter be relieved of the cost of supporting her, in addition to which, he felt fortunate to be gaining a son-in-law of promising quality.

Within the year, Jannet had presented William with his first son, whom they named Joseph after William's father, and Joseph was followed, the next year by Henry. Next came Jane,but sadly, she died within twenty four hours, and only a few hours after she had been baptised. Margaret was born a couple of years afterwards, then John, a year later. John, though was not to survive infancy, and was to die when six months old. It was at this point that William petitioned for an addition to his land tenancy. Initially this was refused, but when William petitioned for permission for an assart, this was subsequently granted in return for a fine. An assart involves the clearance of wooded ground, whereby the tenant must first grub out the trees and shrubs, to make the ground arable. Having done this clearance work, the tenant was required to pay the fine and subsequent rent on the basis of improved value of the land. William applied for and obtained his permission for 3 $\frac{1}{2}$ acres of land on gently rising ground, which plot he named 'Farhill'. The disadvantage was that the land was separated from that which he already held by nearly a mile, with the resulting loss of efficiency in cultivation. However this was a common enough situation, and in addition, William was confident that once he had accomplished the back-breaking task of clearance, and preparation, the land would prove to be considerably more fertile than his acreage by the sea's edge.

He was also conscious that steadily more mouths to feed were appearing in his household at regular intervals. The next to be born was Thomas, and the following year Rowland was baptised, a choice of name not without design. By this time the land at Farhill was in an improved state, and was justifying William's hopes for its fertility. He approached Rowland Finlinson with the proposal that he should yield up the tenancy of his virgate of twenty acres, in return for a further allocation of land for improvement on Farhill. Ten further acres were allocated to him, with the understanding that a further ten acres would be allotted when he had improved the first plot to the satisfaction of the Lord of the manor. Again he would be required to pay an 'entry fine' and to agree to pay rent on the basis of the value of improved land, which improvement would come by his own sweat. In agreeing, the Steward realised that, in return for the tenant's efforts, his landlord would be benefitting by gaining arable land in exchange for woodland. William was in the prime of his life, and felt confident that he could, in the long run, prosper more by this exchange.

And so it proved; within the space of four years, William had brought the ten acres under cultivation, and by then Robert had arrived. Robert was followed, this time after a pause of three years, by Isabel. Susanna was born after two more years. However, Susanna's arrival was accompanied by a tragedy; the sturdy Jannet, who had produced ten children, eight of whom had survived infancy, died giving birth to Susanna. She was forty-two.

William was fortunate that his eldest sons and daughter were old enough to take over a substantial part of the daily tasks of looking after the younger children, of the household chores, and some of the farm duties as well. Nevertheless he realised that it would be unwise and unfair to expect for too long, his children to assume all the adult burdens of responsibility.

Therefore he set about seeking a second wife. He was, after all forty three years old, was still fit and strong, and by local standards for a yeoman, quite successful. After some thought he realised that Rowland Finlinson's eldest daughter, Martha, was the most suitable for consideration. She was thirty-six, unmarried, and therefore likely to consider William's suit more attractive than she might recently have dreamed possible; she was of agreeable disposition, and he pondered, would not harm his relationship with the most influential person on the manor.

Rowland Finlinson was himself quite pleased when William approached him for permission to ask Martha; he had begun to fear that she might spend her whole life 'on the shelf'. There was of course the permission of the Lord of the manor to be sought; but because the Steward's status was not that of a serf, there would be no question of a marriage fine. So, in the event, everyone came out smiling, and shortly afterwards William and Martha were married, and William was able to turn his full attention, once again, to his cultivation.

One morning in the following May, William was busy sowing seeds, with the help of Joseph and Henry, on his land at Farhill. It lay on gently rising ground, and he paused for a moment, straightened his back, and admired the view across the sunlit Solway Firth to the shores of Scotland, and to the mountains rising beyond. As he had many times before, since his own boyhood, he wondered what had become of his brother Henry. Had he been taken to be killed? Or had he been taken by the raiders to spend his life as a slave? William's parents had thought the latter at the time, William remembered. Henry would be 43 now, he reflected.

At that moment he became aware of a commotion of excitement down in the village below him, with several villagers converging on one cottage. Then whilst he was still watching and wondering, a single figure separated itself from the rest, and he recognised it to be Martha, who was running towards him.

Martha was badly out of breath before she drew near, but she gasped "Your brother's back" before collapsing to the ground, completely winded. William unchivalrously dropped his seed pan, and , without a word ran off down the hill, leaving his sons Joseph and Henry to help their stepmother back to her feet. He found his brother, though he scarcely recognised him, in the cottage of a neighbour, surrounded, by now, by most of the villagers. He looked ten years older than his actual age, but apart from that, he appeared lean and fit. William took him next door to his own cottage when the excitement had died down, and Martha sat him down with some food and ale. Only when he had finished, and could draw breath, did William allow him to be plied with questions. During the earlier excited talking at the neighbour's house, it had been gathered that he had been enslaved, but had escaped, two earlier attempts having failed.

Now, surrounded by his brother William, his sister-in-law Martha, and his several nephews and nieces, Henry related his adventures of the past thirty-odd years.

After capture he had been confined and guarded, along with a number of other prisoners, in a building from which he could actually see the English coast, across the Solway. Shortly afterwards, however, they had all been driven, like cattle, along the coast, until they eventually reached a small village with a harbour. This journey lasted two days. No sooner had they flung themselves to the ground in the barn into which they had been herded, than they were roughly roused to their feet, to be paraded before a huge red-haired man, whose language they could not understand. This man inspected the captives briefly, and then turned to one of the captors, who apparently spoke his language. After a brief haggle they seemingly reached agreement, and the captives, without further ado, were roughly driven out of the barn, and across to a small sailing boat, which was tied up alongside the crude breakwater.

After they had been herded aboard, and up into the prow, the red- haired giant came across to the boat, having apparently paid for his human cargo, and, on an order from him, the boat set sail. By now the sun was setting, and having cleared the land, William realised that they were sailing directly towards the sunset.

When daylight returned, Henry recounted, they were close to land, and obviously about to put in to a broad sandy bay. One of the captives hazarded the opinion that this landfall was Ireland. He had heard of this land, many of whose inhabitants had red hair, were wild, hot-tempered, and spoke a strange language. Once ashore they were herded again along a track, until they shortly came in sight of a large village, onto whose green they were herded. Here they were fed, whilst a crowd of villagers gathered around them in a circle, but at a distance. Many of these seemed to be eyeing them, not with curiosity, but almost, it seemed, to be with a professional gaze. This indeed it proved to be, for the captors soon realised that they were being paraded for sale. One of the villagers spoke quite good English, and he confirmed that they were in Ireland. He said that they were to be sold as serfs for farm labouring, and provided they caused no trouble, and worked hard for their owners, they would not find life so different from their previous plight as peasants over in England.

And so, Henry went on, to his attentive audience, he had spent his time as a slave on farms in Ireland. He had belonged to three successive owners, all in the same area, and although he had had to work very hard, and his movements had been closely watched, the first two owners had treated him reasonably well. The last owner, however, had been brutal, and if for any reason he became angry, he would take it out on Henry. This had resolved Henry to attempt to escape. His first two attempts had resulted only in savage beatings from his owner, after the second of which the owner had threatened he would kill Henry if he tried again.

Henry had reflected, after his latest beating, that his usefulness as a slave was bound , eventually, to diminish with age, and that therefore his fate in the hands of this owner was sealed anyway, so escape he must, and the next attempt had to be successful.

On his last attempt he had reached the coast, and he remembered, that on his way he had received shelter from a sympathetic woman for the night. She had given him food, had carefully scanned the scene before he left her barn, and generally seemed to wish to help him escape. He resolved that he would seek her help again, and this time, with her help, would plan his escape from the shores of Ireland more carefully.

He let his next attempt wait for some weeks, until he felt that the owner was less watchful of his movements, and then, one night, he fled the farm again, and made for the cottage of his helper, near the coast. Once there, he was admitted into her home without hesitation; almost as if she had expected his arrival. Whilst she was preparing some food for him, he explained that he needed some sort of boat in which to get safely away. She made no immediate reply, except to say that he should hide again in her barn overnight, and in the morning she would see what she could do. Late in the afternoon she returned to her cottage, and said that she had located a small boat a couple of miles away, on the outskirts of a village, but that it had no sails; he would have to row it. Furthermore she added, she had spotted at least two men, that day, whose preoccupation was evidently to watch out for a fugitive.

On her advice, Henry agreed to remain for a further day, in the hope that any searchers would think that the trail had gone cold. During his stay, Henry learned that his helper was a widow, that her name was Mary, and he realised instinctively that,she was beginning to care for him. He had even briefly considered whether he should dally in her home; she was a pleasant looking woman, and obviously a kind one. However, he knew that he could never feel safe in this land, and that he must go.

So, the next night, after sincerely thanking Mary, he made his careful way to where she had described the boat's location, found it without difficulty, and put to sea, hoping that the currents would enable him to steer in a south-easterly direction, thus avoiding another encounter with the Scots. He was exhausted when after two days and nights, he sighted land. Because he could not see any mountains he felt that he had successfully reached England, and this belief reinforced his waning strength to row some more, and to find his way to the shore. Once there he had a rest from his exertion, before striking inland. Shortly, he reached a village, and discovered from a surprised villager that he was in Lancashire. He had made a good landfall, and was in friendly hands. The villager took him to the house of the Bailiff who, after giving him lodging for the night, sent him on his way homewards. Above all he did not wish Henry to be another burden on his parish!

As soon as possible, William took Henry along to meet the Steward of the manor, Rowland Finlinson, in order to petition for an allocation of land on the manor, for Henry. The steward agreed to ask the Lord when he next saw him, but a few days later sent for Henry and William and told them that he found the Lord of the manor unwilling to make any decisions, excepting those of a routine nature. This was because of a political change which had occurred recently, of which they had heard, that Cumberland had reverted to being a part of the Scottish Kingdom. The Scottish King David was in fact planning to make his seat in Carlisle. This had unsettled many of the Lords, who felt insecure until their new sovereign made his intentions clear.

Rowland Finlinson advised Henry that he would allocate some of the manorial duties to him, and that he should meantime help his brother William in his cultivation. He hoped that the situation would become clarified shortly.

Sure enough, the steward's advice proved to be sound, and it was not long before he was able to persuade his Lord to accede, as a result of which, Henry was soon allocated a few acres close to those of his brother. Furthermore, the political scene changed once more, when in 1157, the county of Cumberland once again became English, under the much stronger sovereignty of Henry of Anjou, (Henry II).

But we jump ahead. In the meantime, since his rehabilitation in Cumberland, Henry had married a young widow, Ann Ritson, from Burgh, and with help from his brother William, and nephews, had built a cottage. Ann had also presented him with two daughters, Ada and Maud, born in 1150 and 1152 respectively. Given that the sorties and raids from across the firth would subside, the prospects for the well-being of these second generation Huntingtons in Cumberland looked quite promising.

****

THE TIME OF THE FIFTH GENERATION - CIRCA 1210.

Occupying the farm at Farhill in Boustead, were William, in his sixties, the grandson of Joseph Huntington, with his wife Jane, also just 60 years old. Of their surviving children, there were two sons, Richard and Stephen, and two daughters, Mary and Margaret. The farm which William cultivated was smaller than the original because that had been split following old William's death, between Joseph and Henry. Since then, the two plots had remained unchanged. The diminution had, however, been mitigated by the use of common land, so that, by evolving much more into mixed farming, with some cattle, some sheep, and also pigs, they were able to live fairly well. The main clouds on the horizon were that the frequency of raiding recently had increased, and that a new Steward had recently been installed on the manor. It had not been long before he had replaced the Bailiff with one of his own choice, and that a much more demanding policy was being fashioned. In particular, the new steward insisted on changing some of the manorial customs, so that fines and charges were levied whenever the opportunity arose. Whereas in earlier times the border tenants had been exempt from most taxes and levies, and indeed still were, now new fines were imposed for collection of dead wood, needed for fuel,milling the grain or the keeping of poultry, as well as other livestock. In fact, any new activity or happening presented the new Lord with an excuse for making a levy. The villagers had no option but to grit their teeth and pay, as the Lord of the manor was in a position wherein his word was law. And so, for the first time on this manor, the previous harmony began to evaporate, and the villagers started to think how they could 'beat the system', rather than cooperate with the heirarchy. In the meantime, William's cousins, grandchildren of Ada Huntington, who had married Joseph Losh, lived in the neighbouring village of Kirkbampton, whilst

William's brother, Thomas, being landless, had gone to Holme Cultram, where an Abbey had been built. Much construction was still under way and there was work for him, at first as a labourer, but as he acquired skills, as a stone mason. When later, William decided to rebuild his cottage at Farhill, the existing one which had been inherited from his grandfather's time, being somewhat decayed, he asked his brother Thomas to obtain permission to return temporarily to Burgh, to help and advise him.

Because a much stricter vigil was maintained by the Steward and Bailiff, to prevent the pilfering of stones from the Wall, they had to use the 'cruck' form of construction, which had the benefit of speed in building. It could be described as one of the earliest attempts to achieve a degree of Prefabricated Building. A series of uprights were needed, and these had to be of Oak, or other hardwood, such as Elm or Ash. These uprights needed to be curved in order to maximise the amount of living space within the building. Thomas's acquired skills enabled him to select suitable trees , from which curved timbers could be obtained. Permission had to be obtained from the Bailiff to fell the required trees, and William was not surprised that the Bailiff extracted the maximum fee from him.

To begin with, a pair of these curved beams was erected at each end of the proposed building, the beams meeting at the ridge to form a gabled shape.These crucks were then fixed together by a collar made of wood. Thomas's skill and experience was useful, in that he knew that the frames were best secured together on the ground, hoisted up into the upright position, and then located in their permanent positions. A ridge tree, consisting of a stout, and straight beam was laid across to unite these end gables. Between these curved uprights were erected more cruck-trussed uprights at intervals, and because it was not possible to find sufficient trees, nearby, suitable to make curved crucks, several of these intermediates had to be formed out of two pieces of jointed timber, in order to provide the curve. Upon these rows of uprights, rafters were laid and fixed along the length of the building, They now had the structure on which to fix the roofing and the walls.

They were able to use the stone from the old building, with which to build solid walls up to about three feet from the ground. From that height to the roof level, the walls were constructed from clay interspersed with rubble and cobble stones, laced with sticks and straw to help bind the material together. This wall, when finished, would be about seven inches thick.

For roofing, purlins of light timber construction were laid along the length of the building on the gable walls, ready for the thatching. Here again, Thomas recommended that the most suitable sedge material could be obtained from Sebergham, and together they set off for the few miles, with a borrowed cart, to choose and obtain the material. In common with the practice at the time, there were no windows to the new building, nor was there a chimney, so smoke had to find its way out via the badly fitting doorways.

These conditions of living, which we would find intolerable, were common, and Langland, of Piers Plowman fame, vividly described them when he pictured "the peasant, bleary-eyed, or worse, and hoarse with the smoke and smolder, so that he coughs and curses that God may chastise those whose business it is to bring in dry wood, or at least to blow it until it is blazing".The floor was of trodden earth, with straw used to maintain some semblance of cleanliness.

William and Mary were well pleased with their new home; it promised to be dryer than their previous cottage, and it certainly had more valuable room, comprising the living room, a bedroom in the loft space reached by a ladder, and a third room for housing their livestock when necessary. Not only were they delighted, but the villagers were impressed by the skill and speed with which the new cottage had been built. Thomas agreed to remain at Boustead, when the Steward put it to him that there was plenty of work on the manor to engage his building skills. This, and the likelihood of work from other admiring villagers, seemed to open up a promising vista for him back in his home village.

On several occasions Thomas had noticed a young widow, and he had seen also that she had noticed him. She had a small holding of about 3 acres just outside the village, which she did not appear to be able to cultivate very successfully. She had a small child, which occupied her to the detriment of the land.

Thomas went to see her in her cottage, and offered to do some work on it between his building and repair jobs, which she shyly accepted. Her name was Margrett, and within a few weeks Thomas and she were married. Her little son, George, was delighted to have a father once more. So Thomas became a yeoman as well as a builder, and in the ensuing years he and Margrett added to their family with two more sons, Henry and William, as well as two daughters, Margaret and Eleanor. Thus was another dynasty started on its way, as well as a promising new occupation, especially when William's son Richard announced that he too was going to be a builder, like his uncle, when he grew up...........

****

THE TIME OF THE TENTH GENERATION - CIRCA 1310

The manor at Burgh had just changed hands, and the new Lord of the Manor was Robert de Trivers, who had taken it over from the Meschins family. Nobody liked change, because, whilst some people might complain about the customs which prevailed, these seemed bearable when a possibility of change arose. It was bad enough for them to have to pay a fine to the Lord on his taking over, but at least that was a forseen happening. By now there were several family groups of Huntingtons in the district, all descendants of the original settlers. These relations were well used to helping one another whenever necessary, and this fact gave them all some confidence with which to face life's problems. They could help each other at times of the year when the pressure of work was heaviest, such as at haymaking time.

A change which was in the process of developing, was the growth of the demand for woollen cloth. The Abbey, a few miles away was taking advantage of this trend, developing its sheep pasturing, and becoming quite important in the business of spinning and weaving.So well developed had it become in recent times, that it was nowadays taking supplies of wool from other nearby sources, which included Burgh, as well as other parishes in Allerdale. Given a steady and rising demand, the villagers increased their own flocks of sheep, and within a few years, some of them had become over-dependent on the Abbey for custom. The growth of the industry in Cumbria had been at the expense of towns engaged in the textile business in the south. This was because the old crude methods of thickening the cloth had been overtaken by the Fulling Mills, driven by water wheels in fast moving streams and rivers, which sprang up in numbers, in Cumbria.

In the preceding ten years or so, the border raids had increased, not only in frequency, but also in strength and intensity. The reason is to be found in the policy of King Edward I. A successful king in both domestic and foreign policy, he had, after his conquest and pacification of Wales, set out to repeat the exercise in Scotland. After initial success, which nearly brought him triumph, he was foiled by the uprising led by William Wallace, and his army was defeated by Robert Bruce, in 1314, at Bannockburn. Retaliatory raids, particularly after King Edward died in 1307, at Burgh-by-Sands, followed thereafter, and continued in a renewed intensity for long afterwards. Hatred and bitterness between the two sides mounted, and really did not subside until the beginning of the seventeenth century, when after Queen Elizabeth's reign, the two countries were to unite under one crown. Paradoxically, despite this fierce animosity, Scottish emigrants filtered across the border, to settle in Cumberland, during this whole period of border tension, and the English authorities generally behaved tolerantly toward this. On the other hand, many inhabitants of Cumberland came to resent this peaceful invasion, because it frequently happened that these immigrants ousted many farmers and yeomen from their land holdings, by offering higher rents. There were many, also, who suspected that the immigrants included some who acted as spies and guides to the raiders, and also some who gave shelter to these invaders.

In consequence, the villagers, all along the border, were required to give much more duty as border guards, watchmen, or at the Beacon points, which had been set up to spread warnings of danger round the country. By this time, early in the fourteenth century, the Huntington families had dispersed to other nearby parishes. This became necessary when parents died; their children would each inherit strips of their land, and as this process continued, each generation was left with ever smaller holdings, insufficient to support their families. This meant that the peasants would be forced to become labourers, working for a wage for somebody else, cultivating their own little strip in their spare time. The alternative was to move to another parish nearby, where it might still be possible to secure a tenancy. To the south of them was the vast forest land, and particularly in the forest of Westward, encroachments were being allowed by men who were prepared to undertake the back-breaking work of an assart; the clearing of scrubland and woodland, and its husbanding into productive, arable land. Now there were Huntingtons in Westward, as well as Thursby, Great Orton, and Kirkbampton. Later in the century, in 1348, in addition to their problems, of perpetual border raids, excessive taxation, as they thought, by the Lords of the manors, occasional periods of hunger, caused by bad weather and crop failures, and very high infant mortality, another tragedy lay in wait for them; the Bubonic plague. Some of us might recall the childhood game and chant which included: "Atishoo, Atishoo, we all fall down", which probably we didn't realise had derived from the scourge called 'The Black Death', alias the Bubonic and Pneumonic Plagues. This swept into England from Asia, via Europe, and, as the verse suggests, at one moment a victim felt fit, and in a very short time he would be dead, having had no warning symptoms. The Black Death decimated whole populations, and in England, is thought to have carried off nearly half of the populace. Worse was to come, for a second outbreak occurred in 1361/2, and although Cumberland was not as badly afflicted as most parts of the country, an analysis of burial records for those periods of the disease, compared with periods preceding and following them, indicates that the deaths caused by the plague amounted to nearly thirty per cent of the people. The disease was nondiscriminatory and killed holy people, nobles and peasants alike. Country districts, as well as towns suffered alike, though the coastal area of the Solway Plain seems to have been least affected, along with the mountainous districts.

Fortunately then, the families in and near Burgh by Sands escaped lightly, but those families living even a few miles inland, including Great Orton, Thursby and Westward, were thinned out quite savagely. A third outbreak burst out in 1369, but this affected mainly districts to the west of Cumberland. Presumably those who had survived the earlier ravages had some kind of immunity from that particular strain. It took a long time for the country generally, to recover from the setback, and the all-important business of growing or rearing enough food, was retarded severely.

Later in the century, the conflicts between England and Scotland, which hitherto had mainly been raids, flared into real war, and in 1380 Carlisle was besieged, until an English army relieved the city. The villagers in nearby settlements were living in a constant state of anxiety, and those who owned livestock took to keeping them in their homes at nights. Much of the surrounding countryside was devastated by the invaders, as well as by the relieving soldiers, who would help themselves without restraint by their officers. The monks in the Abbey at Holme Cultram actually paid the Earl of Douglas a £200 ransom to prevent his countrymen from causing destruction to their crops and property. Twice, within the following few years, Carlisle was again besieged, and much destruction suffered in the country nearby, and the culmination came in 1388 with the destruction of the town of Appleby. An uneasy peace only came in 1394, with a truce signed between England , Scotland, and their allies, France. This was confirmed by a treaty of peace signed in 1401, though it was honoured mainly in the breach, for within a year the Scots had to be driven back from Carlisle once again, and depredations continued sporadically for some time.

To end this troubled fourteenth century on a slightly lighter note: The minutes of Leet Courts largely deal with petty infractions of the Lords' rights, and record fines for peasants found guilty of stealing wood from the forest, and, the most heinous of local crimes,of hunting in the Lord's forests. It is quite common to come across records wherein priests and gentlemen were arraigned for similar offences of hunting without leave in the forest. It was amusing, therefore, to read, in 'Prelates and People of the Lake Counties', by C.M.L.Bouch, of Bishop Appleby's reaction in 1374, when he heard that poachers had been at work in his Park at Rose. He excommunicated those 'sons of iniquity' who had broken into his park, and taken his deer with dogs, nets, and other engines, so that the deer were totally destroyed.......... It was alright for some!

Nothing has been mentioned so far, about education. This is because, for all but a very few, none was available. The Reverend C.M.L. Bouch, in his "Prelates and People of the Lake Counties" wrote that the first school mentioned, was that of Carlisle in 1188. Some schools existed, because in 1259, injunctions were sent to parish priests near the cities and castles, on the matter of their administration to scholars. Penrith had a school at an early date; a schoolmaster was licenced to teach there in 1340, and there is evidence that a school existed in Cockermouth in that century, as did one at Appleby. A school at Kendal was founded in the sixteenth century, and so was one at Brough. The visitation roll for the diocese of Carlisle in 1573 shews schoolmasters at Penrith, Brough, Appleby, Barton, Morland, Crosthwaite, Aspatria and Westward. About the same time, in the Chester Deaneries, the 1578 visitation shews schoolmasters at St.Bees,

Cockermouth, Lorton, Bootle, Dalton, Ulverston, Barbon, Beetham, and Kendal.

From there, the founding of schools grew in pace, with schools at Kirkby Stephen, 1566, Keswick, 1571, Blencow 1577/8, Urswick 1580, St.Bees 1583, Hawkshead 1585, Kirkby Lonsdale 1591, Stainmore 1594, Dean 1596, Crosby Garrett about 1600, Ireleth 1608, Bridekirk 1609, Bromfield 1612, Old Hutton 1613, and so the numbers grew as the seventeenth century progressed. The Cumbrians valued, and wished for Education with an intensity matching that of the Scots across the border, and whereas the Scots enacted an Education Act in the middle of the eighteenth century, the Cumbrians had to wait until 1870, when the English Education Act came onto the Statute Book. .

BELOW: ST. MICHAEL'S CHURCH
BURGH-BY-SANDS   PHOTOGRAPHED BY KINDNESS OF MR WILSON SWAN

THIS WAS BUILT WITH TWO PURPOSES IN MIND FIRSTLY AS A CHURCH, SECONDLY AS A WATCHTOWER.

ORIGINALLY IT HAD TWO TOWERS WHOSE WALLS WERE SIX OR SEVEN FEET THICK

53. Cruck construction
a. diagram to show how roof loads are carried by cruck frame to the ground
b. two-bay cruck-framed building with closed crucks (1), open cruck (2), cruck blade (3), tie beam (4), collar (5), ridge purlin (6), side purlin (7), wall plate (8)
c. diagram to show sequence of rearing crucks
d. full cruck with side purlins carried on blocks, blades rising from ground level
e. full cruck with side purlins carried on outer blades (9)
f. raised cruck with blades supported on the wall
g. upper cruck with blades rising from the lower tie beam
h. upper cruck with collar
i. yoke at ridge
j. blades halves and crossed at ridge
k. ridge purlin carried on king block on saddle
l. collar yoke
m. blades halves or tenoned at ridge
n. gable end of a ridge purlin carried on a short king post supported on a spreader and steadied by curved braces
o. and p. side purlins trenched into blades with straight or curved braces (after Moorhouse)
q. cruck tie locating wall plate which is supported by wall

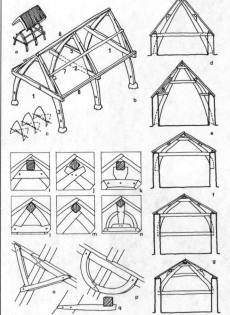

ABOVE: CRUCK-BUILT
BARN AT GREAT ORTON
BCHME ©

LEFT:DETAILS OF CRUCK
FORMS OF CONSTRUCTION
REPRODUCED BY THE
KIND PERMISSION OF
PROF.R.W.BRUNSKILL.
AUTHOR OF VERNACULAR
ARCHITECTURE OF THE
LAKE COUNTIES.

THE TIME OF THE FIFTEENTH GENERATION - CIRCA 1420

Only a man harrowing clods
In a slow silent walk With an old horse that stumbles and nods
Half asleep as they stalk.

Only thin smoke without flame
From the heaps of couch-grass Yet this will go onward the same
Though dynasties pass.

(Thomas Hardy's poem, in In Time of "The Breaking of Nations")

The preceding century, many of whose adversities continued into the fifteenth century, had devastated the county, and in particular, the region surrounding Carlisle. There had been no true let-up in the border conflicts, despite truces, peace treaties, and the earnest efforts of Commissioners sent to the border to try and placate the inhabitants. Too much bitterness prevailed from loss of lives, and the destruction of property.

A whole family of Huntingtons, along with many other villagers, lost their lives in 1425, when a large marauding band of Scots, out foraging during a siege of Carlisle, descended on the hamlets of Cardewleas, and Nealehouse. Angered at the inability or refusal of the villagers to reveal the whereabouts of their stocks of food, prudently hidden away, they ruthlessly put to the sword without mercy or discrimination, all who failed to flee. Having 'liberated' any livestock found, they then fired both hamlets, before returning to their boring task of investing the city.

The plagues also continued to take their toll. The worst of the epidemic had played itself out, but minor outbreaks continued to flare up, and to reap their grisly harvest of death. It was believed that the disease was caused by bad air, and this belief was reinforced by those living on the immediate coast along the Solway. They had escaped the worst onslaughts of the disease, so the disease-carrying rats which abounded everywhere, escaped the blame, and no serious attempt, on acount of their particular threat, was made to eradicate them.

The brothers Edward, and George Huntington, of East Curthwaite, fell victim to the renewed epidemic of Pneumonic Plague, which occurred in 1433/34. This was the deadliest and swiftest killer of the varieties of the Black Death; so swift that neither of them lived to witness the fate of their wives and small children, who had quickly succumbed. This visitation departed as quickly as it had arrived, leaving yet another village short of able-bodied folk.

The Seneschal, or Steward of the manor, had a problem on his hands, in that the manor faced a busy spring and summer of sowing, haymaking, and harvesting, in addition to the lambing, and care of the livestock generally. He solved it by visiting his counterparts at Great Orton and Burgh. He had no success at Orton, where the Steward was unwilling to spare any peasants. At Burgh, he had more success, because their losses had been light, and the Steward knew of some young men, younger sons without any prospect of inheriting land, who might be willing to move. Indeed he privately suspected that they might in any case abscond to shift for themselves. So he thought that he might as well try to profit from the situation, by agreeing to release some men in return for appropriate recompense.

Money changed hands, and as it happened, two of the young men, both with wives, were Huntingtons - Robert and his cousin John. These 'migrants' were induced by the promise of being allowed to take over the tenancies of villagers who had lost their lives. John was given the tenancy of twenty acres of land at How Ridge. It was a promising piece of land, but there remained quite a lot of clearance and preparation, of nearly half it before it could be brought to full cultivation. Previously it had been an assart, an encroachment on the forest only partly completed. Robert Huntington took over the tenancy of a smaller plot of about 12 acres, at Evening Hill. All of the incoming families were allowed rights on the common land, and all of them, in addition to accepting militia duties, and 'watch' duties, were required to undertake some 'boon' duties at Haymaking and Harvest times for the manor. These, however, were not very onerous requirements, in keeping with those of most tenants of the manor.

Another migration from the coastal area near to Burgh, was that of Rowland Huntington, who, with his wife Jane, and along with other land hungry villagers, moved to Papcastle, near to Cockermouth. This area, though still subjected occasionally to raids from across the firth, was considerably quieter. Because it had suffered only lightly from Scottish depredations, and from the Black Death, it was a great deal more prosperous as a result. The weaving industry was thriving, and a trade was beginning to build up via some excellent small ports adjacent to Cockermouth. So whilst continuing their traditional agricultural lifestyle, these people supplemented their livelihood by entering the weaving business, an occupation in which the whole family could participate - wives, down to even quite young children. Fell sheep were grazed in large numbers on the nearby Derwent Fells, and the weavers would travel, with a jointly owned cart, up-river to the Lorton Vale, to fetch the wool from the farmers, returning to weave it into cloth for sale onwards, and then repeating the process. By this means a good deal of trust developed between these participants in the wool trade; the sheep farmer, the weaver, and the merchant. It was not to be long, having built up their private little network, before some of the weavers moved up the Vale, and installed themselves in situ for their weaving, thus saving a journey from the producer to weaver.

This is a period of which we know very little, because the records left and kept preserved for us are so scanty. They were troublesome times, when people had to be pre-occupied with the business of survival. The population, which prior to the fourteenth century, had been expanding rapidly, had shrunk significantly, largely, as we have seen because of the plague. Thereafter growth of the population was static, or very slow for a long time.

THE TIME OF THE TWENTIETH GENERATION - CIRCA 1536

King Henry VIII had been on the throne of England by now, for some 27 years, and his reign had ushered in some improvements in the condition of the land; some greater prosperity, and , with it some hopes that the lot of the peasant would be improved also. The reign also had much turbulence in store, which was going to affect everyone. Not least were the religious conflicts, which culminated in the Reformation of the Church, the abolition of the monasteries, and schism between the respective adherants of the new Church of England, and those who clung to the Roman Catholic faith.

The smaller monasteries were the first to fall victim of abolition, but the turn of Holme Cultram Abbey came in 1538. The inhabitants petitioned that the Abbey Church should be preserved on the grounds that it served as their parish church, as well as a place of refuge and defence against the scots. This petition was granted, and the Abbey remained as one of only four which survived the Reformation.

Manorial life continued, and these political and ecclesiastical events came into the awareness of the peasants and yeomen farmers only distantly. Here follows a typical record of one of the Manorial Courts:

WESTWARDE; COURT HELD THERE ON THE 27TH DAY OF JULY, IN THE 17TH YEAR OF THE REIGN KING HENRY VIII, IN THE NAME OF THE AFORESAID FEOFFORS.

By the oath of William Scott, William Ashbrig, Jnr., Richard Wattson, Robert Geffrey Adam Ismay, Robert Jackson, John Dowson, William Thomson, Adam Williamson, John Tiffen.

FORESTERS' PRESENTMENTS

First they present James Abbot, of Greynrig for two horsedraughts of Alder. fine 2d. Also they present William Aykhed of Flosh, for one cartload of Wattling. 2d Also they present Thomas Lyghtfut of Kirkland, for one cartload of deadwood. 1d Also they present John Jackson of Brigham for two cartloads of garthing. 2d . . . To the affeerers of the court Thomas Nicholson, forester, presents James Ashbrig for three swine trespassing on the lord's several land. fine 6d

WESTWARDE: COURT HELD THERE ON THE 4TH DAY OF OCTOBER, IN THE 17TH YEAR OF THE REIGN OF KING HENRY VIII, IN THE NAME OF THE AFORESAID FEOFFORS.

List of Jurors given.

It was found by the inquisition of William Herryson and his fellows that John Darnetone (or Darvetone), canon of Carlisle did hunt with many dogs and servants in the lord's forest there, and killed nothing - on two occasions with divers gentlemen in his company. Also they say that William Musgrave, Knight, Thomas Blennerhasset, of Carlisle, gentleman, Edward Aglionby of the same place, Gentleman and Antony Musgrave, canon, did hunt in the lord's forest with harriers and killed there one doe on the 24th day of July in the present year.. . . . Also they present John Huntington for 1 alder .Disallowed for uncertainty

. . . Also they say that John Anderson, a forester, found a hunter with his dogs, to wit Canon Antony Musgrave, and did not catch him, nor did he report about him, but unlawfully concealed the matter, on the 20th day of September. Also they present the wife of Jenkyn Loshe for one stray dog worrying sheep. (to be put out of the way).

Also they say that Richard Scott has not removed his house as the Seneschal ordered him- nothing in penalty because it was presented before the lord's commissioner that the said house is not rented, nor parcel of any holding. Referred to the lord's council.

Note the almost audible change into tones of respect when reference was made to persons from the higher orders. We presume that it was the dog, not the wife of Jenkyn Loshe, to be put out of the way. As can be seen from the above typical selection from the records, the manors continued their oppressive exploitation of their citizens, serfs or tenants.

This century, like the fifteenth before it, was to be dominated by the twin scourges of war and disease, to which latter we should perhaps add famine.

Sporadic raiding persisted throughout the period, and although places as far south as Appleby were subjected to attacks, it was the real borderlands which bore the brunt of the incursions. The Solway firth was little protection, as, at low tide it could be forded by experienced men, and it was only if a western gale developed that they could be at risk. Likewise, the land frontiers north and east of Carlisle, had scant protection from the rivers Esk and Liddel, which were easily fordable. Protection was supposed to be given by a series of manned watch places, with beacons to be lit in order to warn the surrounding countryside. The warnings given would mobilise the militia, under the control of the Warden of the West Marches.

The Calendar of Border Papers, 1580/81, records for the several parishes their liability to mobilise militia men, subject to be called out, naming, for the Leath Ward, 83 bowmen, and 2000 men armed with steel coats, caps, spears or lances; a few had guns; In Carlisle, the musters numbered 374 horsemen, in addition to the foot militia. In Northumberland and Cumberland combined, the musters totalled over 20000, comprising 7000 horsemen, and 13000 foot militia. Artillery was kept at Carlisle. In Westward, there were Huntingtons listed in the rolls, as there were also in East Curthwaite. The report on the available mustering in Burgh-by-Sands was less optimistic: "Theire is foure surnames theire, Liddalles, Glasters, Huntingtons, and Hodgesons, but theire is not many of none of them" The report goes on to list the several surnames of the borderers of Scotland, and their dwellings, who were known to be regular invaders, listing the Johnsons of Sark, a Kinmont, and about 100 Armstrongs, in Boneshowe, the Irvings, in Liddesdale, more Armstrongs, and in Dumfries, Lord Maxwell and about 1000 Maxwells

West of Burgh-by-Sands lay the Holme Lordship. South of Holme lay the Allerdale, whose inhabitants were liable for 'March Days', or when sent for by the warden. South of Burgh were the Barony of Wigton, and the Forest of Westward, under the Earl of Northumberland's steward, who had to lead the inhabitants in case of service, and still further south was the Caldbeck lordship, whose tenants mustered under a bailiff when the warden sent for them. Between Caldbeck and Penrith lay Greystoke, whose tenants were used for 'March Days', and for 'watch and search'. Between Westward and the Inglewood Forest lay Sebergham, under the Queen's bailiff, who led the tenants to the numbers required by the warden, when sent for. Dalston's service was at Sebergham, 'But more to follow affrays, and aid Burgh'.In the Forest of Inglewood, which stretched from Penrith to Carlisle, its tenants had to comply with the instructions of the warden for any general or particular service he required.

In this century there was no real let-up in the raids across the border; they usually came at night, and the long dark winter nights were the favourite times. It was reported in 1593, that people living within twenty miles of Carlisle were so fearful of the raids that they routinely took to keeping their cattle in their houses by night.

During her reign, Queen Elizabeth had enacted that, upon her death, the crowns of England and Scotland should be united under one sovereign. But nevertheless, as her long reign dragged on, the raids continued unabated, slowed only, it seemed, by the effects of the plague. The Queen died in 1603, and although the raids gradually petered out, thievery continued after the Union - within the borders as well as across them.

It is interesting to note, before turning to disease and famine in the sixteenth century, the soldier's ration, as stated in 'The Last Years of a Frontier', by D.L.W.Tough.: 12 ounces of bread; 3 pints of beer; 12 ounces of cheese; 4 ounces of butter; or 1 ½ lbs of beef, instead of the butter and cheese.

These were the stipulated rations, but whether these were regularly provided, we do not know. Certainly they would seem like a feast to a contemporary peasant, who did not often manage to include meat in his diet!

Plague epidemics persisted throughout the siteenth century, with heavy death rates; particularly bad epidemics broke out in 1568, 1569, 1570, and in 1577, where, for instance 38 people died in Hawkshead. There was more in 1588 1593, and then the severest epidemic occurred in 1597/98. In that year the parish registers in Penrith recorded 608 deaths, whereas a normal number of deaths for that period would have been 60. An entry in Jefferson's Leath Ward, page 19, recorded :

"A sore plague in Richmond, Kendal, Penreth, Carliell, Apulbie, and other places in Westmorland and Cumberland, in the year of our Lord 1598..............................." CWAAS XI 158-186, by Henry Barnes.

Inevitably wierd options for avoidance of or treatment for the plague, were canvassed by the soothsayers, one of the most strange, to our current beliefs anyway, was that SMOKING IS GOOD FOR YOUR HEALTH, and there were reports of pupils at Eton College being chastised for refusing to take their regular smoke.

In these instances, mentions of the Plague are not likely to have referred to the Bubonic or Pneumonic Plague, but are thought much more probably to have been epidemics of Typhus. In fact, as Mr. A.B.Appleby suggested, in his "Famine in Tudor and Stuart England", the common name for Typhus was 'Famine Fever', because conditions of starvation were frequently associated with the disease. He drew the distinction that the crisis of 1588 was almost certainly Typhus, but that the crisis of 1597/8 was largely starvation leading to the disease. It is difficult for us, in modern times, to associate famine with our country, and in particular with such fertile areas as the Solway Plain, and the Eden Valley. We tend to assocaite such crises with far off areas, ususally drought-ridden such as East Africa, or Asia.

There were many contributory causes which affected England at this time, and top of the list of culprits must be the epidemics of disease which had regularly assaulted the country, thinning the populations, and weakening the survivors. In Cumberland, the wars and border conflicts must have reduced agricultural effort considerably, both by death and by frequent absences from the farms. The arrangements of the farming lands went counter to efficient farming, and therefore to adequate food production; the parcelling of the land out to the sons, when the farmer died, led to tiny holdings. Each strip was not necessarily contiguous with the rest of the holding, which did not help efficiency. And of course, the produce, when harvested, had to be divided between the Landlord, the Church, the State and the tenant.

And finally, bad weather could severely set back agriculture, by damaging or destroying crops, and killing livestock. The second half of the sixteenth century witnessed the beginnings of a sea change in weather patterns, bringing long bitterly cold spells.and cold springs. Although weather records are not available for that period,they are from the beginning of the seventeenth century, and we can see that the phase of colder winters and springs continued.

It was in the second half of this century that Cumberland saw the beginnings of Land Enclosure; in 1569 the first enclosures were initiated by the Steward of Westward Forest, and although this had some very painful consequences for the peasant, in the short term, the policy was, in the long run, to lead to much more efficient use of farm lands

All of these troubles and problems must have made life more difficult than we can imagine, and people in Cumberland will have looked forward with yearning for at least an end of border troubles, as the seventeenth century was ushered in.

THE TIME OF THE TWENTY FIFTH GENERATION - CIRCA 1640

With the Stuart Kings on the throne, the seventeenth century began with peace at least on the borders. Epidemics of disease had broken out in 1623, bringing more deaths, followed by more famine. The population, which had increased gently, in spite of the epidemics,in the latter half of the sixteenth century, now declined between 1603 and 1640. It was to start to rise slowly again from 1641 onward, though Carlisle, Keswick,Cockermouth, and St.Bees had epidemics in 1645, 1646, 1647, and 1650, respectively. Penrith suffered an outbreak of Smallpox in 1656. The county was therefore kept in a state of alarm for all of this time. It was the towns which became victims on these occasions however.

The weather continued to make farming life difficult. At least once in every ten years, there seemed to be long hard wintry frosts, and late springs. These would bring death to the sheep and lambs, and hardship, if not ruin to the farmers. Crops would be set back if not destroyed. In 1607-8, for instance there was frost in Cumberland from 3rd November until 6th March.

The dominant political feature of this century was the Rebellion. Although King Charles kept his head in place until 1649, the preceding decade was one of strife and internal war, as Oliver Cromwell sought to depose the King, and to bring in a new order .

Apart from a mustering of the militia for the defence of Carlisle in 1638, the war did not touch most of Cumbria until 1645, when Royalist forces were besieged in Carlisle, and held out bravely, until famine forced their surrender. The soldiers capitulated with honour, and were treated well, but it is an unrecorded fact that it had been the ordinary peasants, who had suffered from the warring which swept over their lands.

Carlisle was under attack again in 1648, which changed hands once more, but only briefly. The rebels eventually prevailed, and the King was beheaded. In Carlisle the Cathedral was badly damaged by the victorious troops. The most significant effect of the establishment of the Commonwealth was that numerous clergymen were ejected from their churches, many of whom subsequently became teachers. The control of the parishes, and we must remember how big a part these had played in the governance of the people, was divided between the various religious sects - Independents and Presbyterians, until, to quote the Reverend C.M.L.Bouch, in his "Prelates and People of the Lake Counties", " a religious genius appeared and emptied the churches of all of them". To continue to quote him : "George Fox, in a few years was almost universally accepted as the sovereign pontiff of Cumberland".

During the next few years, George Fox criss-crossed Cumberland and

Westmorland, (in the course of which he met and married a Westmerian lady, Margaret Fell), preaching to crowded audiences. The Religious Society of Friends, to use the correct title for the Quakers, was to outlast the Commonwealth, which ended in 1660, with the crowning of King Charles II, Cromwell having died in 1658. The Church and Episcopy were restored, the ejected clergy returned to their livings, and one of the longest-lasting consequences of the Rebellion was the loss for ever of Church records for a period of years.

The chapters which follow introduce the several family groups of Huntingtons, which had survived the happenings of the previous centuries, and which were revealed by the resumption of the keeping of Church and Parish records in the 1660s. Before that period, and particularly for the period of the Rebellion, our only guides are copies of wills which may have been made by our ancestors, and preserved since then, and various other documents or records, which we may be fortunate enough to discover. These, by their nature though, only might give us a brief snapshot, at a given moment, of events, but by no means will provide a continuous story of their lives.

As an example of this, given below is a list of Huntington wills from the sixteenth century. The location given for the testators indicates the branch of the Huntingtons, described in the following chapters, to which they belonged, as well as their immediate relations. There is not enough information though to plot an accurate line to us, their descendants.

YEAR	TESTATOR	LEGATEES
1574	John Huntington of Thursby	Son John, daughter Jennet
1574	Christopher H.of Kirkbampton	Robert H. also Thomas Threlkeld Bailiff of Burgh-by-Sands
1575	Edmund H. of Kirkbampton	Daughter Agnes,& Thos.Twentyman
1576	Martin H. of "	Wife Janet, sons John & Robert
1580	Margaret of Westward	John & Jane,Stepchildren etc.
1585	John of "	Eldest son John, daughter Jane Wife Janet children Robt.& Will
1586	William of "	Wife Janet, dtrs Janet & Margt.
1593	Thomas of Orton. Clarke	Brothers John Robt.Edwd,sister Jane, etc 1596 Edmund of Kirkbampton Robert,Edmund,Edwd,Agnes,Willm.
1599	David of Orton	Sons John,Rowland,dtr Agnes Blayne.
1599	Robert of Kirkbampton	John Edwd.,Robt.,dtr Mabel.

Note: We have also copies of 18 Huntington wills from the 17thcentury, each of them, like those above, tantalisingly leaving clues to their immediate relationships, but nothing more. Some of the wills, and their accompanying inventories do however, provide an interesting insight into their lives

Here is a resume of the bequests made by Thomas Huntington of Orton, Clarke, in 1593: "To my brother's son John, one doublet of cloth, not yet made,one gilt dagger, one pair of breeches, and six pounds in money. I give to

Robert his brother,seven pounds to be paid when he completes his apprenticeship. I give to Edward, their brother, seven pounds to be paid when he reaches the age of 21 years. I give to Jane, their sister six oxen and all the fodder, and four pounds, and so on.........(Note: £1 = £50 of today's money)

CHAPTER TWO

CHART NO.1
TWO FAMILIES OF QUAKER HUNTINGTONS IN CUMBRIA

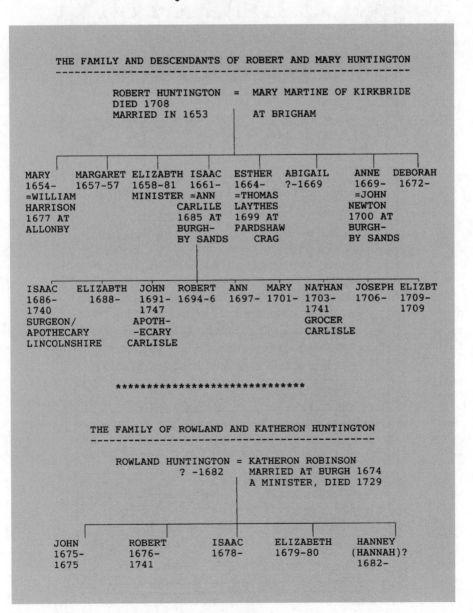

```
THE FAMILY AND DESCENDANTS OF ROBERT AND MARY HUNTINGTON
----------------------------------------------------------

          ROBERT HUNTINGTON  =  MARY MARTINE OF KIRKBRIDE
          DIED 1708
          MARRIED IN 1653       AT BRIGHAM


MARY     MARGARET ELIZABTH ISAAC   ESTHER  ABIGAIL    ANNE   DEBORAH
1654-    1657-57  1658-81  1661-   1664-   ?-1669     1669-  1672-
=WILLIAM          MINISTER =ANN    =THOMAS            =JOHN
HARRISON                   CARLILE LAYTHES            NEWTON
1677 AT                    1685 AT 1699 AT            1700 AT
ALLONBY                    BURGH-  PARDSHAW           BURGH-
                          BY SANDS  CRAG             BY SANDS


ISAAC    ELIZABTH JOHN    ROBERT  ANN     MARY   NATHAN  JOSEPH ELIZBT
1686-    1688-    1691-   1694-6  1697-   1701-  1703-   1706-  1709-
1740              1747                           1741            1709
SURGEON/          APOTH-                         GROCER
APOTHECARY        -ECARY                         CARLISLE
LINCOLNSHIRE      CARLISLE


        *******************************


THE FAMILY OF ROWLAND AND KATHERON HUNTINGTON
----------------------------------------------------

          ROWLAND HUNTINGTON = KATHERON ROBINSON
                  ? -1682      MARRIED AT BURGH 1674
                               A MINISTER, DIED 1729


     JOHN        ROBERT      ISAAC    ELIZABETH   HANNEY
     1675-       1676-       1678-    1679-80     (HANNAH)?
     1675        1741                             1682-
```

A

COLLECTION

OF THE

SUFFERINGS

Of the PEOPLE called

QUAKERS,

FOR THE

Testimony of a Good Conscience,

FROM

The TIME of their being first distinguished by that NAME in the Year 1650, to the TIME of the *Act,* commonly called the *Act of Toleration,* granted to *Protestant* Dissenters in the first Year of the Reign of King WILLIAM *the Third* and Queen Mary, in the Year 1689.

Taken from ORIGINAL RECORDS *and other* AUTHENTICK ACCOUNTS,

By JOSEPH BESSE.

VOLUME I.

JOHN xv. 20. *The Servant is not greater than the* LORD : *If they have persecuted me, they will also persecute you.*

PSAL. xxxiv. 19. *Many are the Afflictions of the Righteous, but the* LORD *delivereth him out of them all.*

PSAL. xii. 5. *For the Oppression of the Poor, for the Sighing of the Needy, now will I arise, saith the* LORD : *I will set him in Safety from him that puffeth at him.*

L O N D O N :

Printed and Sold by LUKE HINDE, at the BIBLE in *George-Yard, Lombard-Street,* M,DCC,LIII.

CHAP. 9. *of the* People *called* QUAKERS. 127

CHAP IX.

CUMBERLAND.

ANNO 1653.

GEORGE FOX, for preaching the Truth in the great Worſhip-houſe at *Carliſle*, after the Prieſt had ended his Sermon, and for witneſſing a good Confeſſion before the Magiſtrates and People there, was impriſoned ſeven Weeks, ſometimes among Thieves and Murderers. *G. Fox impriſoned.*

Robert *Withers*, for aſking the Prieſt of *Aketon* a religious Queſtion after Sermon, was impriſoned at *Carliſle* one Month ; as was George *Bewly* for accompanying him. Robert *Huntington*, for Preaching at *Carliſle*, was impriſoned *three Months*, and *James Noble*, for the ſame Cauſe, *nine Weeks*. *Sundry others impriſoned.*

Robert *Withers*, Thomas *Rawlinſon*, John *Stubbs*, and Thomas *Gwin*, for declaring againſt falſe Worſhip at the Steeple-houſe in *Coldbeck*, were inhumanly treated by the rude People, one of them being knocked down, and much of their Blood ſpilled on the Place.

John *Martin*, for teſtifying againſt the Prieſt of *Kirkbride*, whom he met in the Fields, and calling him by his proper Name, *viz. an Hireling*, was committed to Priſon.

ANNO 1654. Thomas *Stubbs* was concerned to go into the Steeple-houſe at *Deane*, where, when the Prieſt had done, he ſaid, *Thou daubeſt the People up with untempered Mortar* ; whereupon the Prieſt bid his Hearers *fight for the Goſpel* ; they fell violently upon *Stubbs* and ſome of his Friends, tore their Clothes, and beat them cruelly. The Prieſt's Son in particular ſorely bruiſed the Face of Richard *Richardſon*. After which two Juſtices ſent *Stubbs* to Priſon, but conſcious of the Wrong they did him, writ his *Mittimus* and *Diſcharge* both on one Paper ; this furniſhed the Goaler with a Claim for Fees, under Pretence of which he kept him fourteen Weeks in Priſon. *T. Stubbs abuſed.*

Peter *Head*, for teſtifying to the Truth, in the ſame Place, was impriſoned fourteen Weeks in a cloſe Room among Felons in the Heat of Summer ; and John *Head*, for delivering ſome Queries to the Prieſt of *Deane* at his own Houſe, was impriſoned fourteen Weeks. John *Slee*, for reproving a Prieſt at *Griſdale*, was kept a cloſe Priſoner among Felons two Months. Alſo Katharine *Fell*, for aſking a Prieſt, *whether he did witneſs what he ſpake to the People*, was kept in Priſon nineteen Weeks, having a young Child ſucking at her Breaſt. *Impriſonment of P. Head and others.*

Thomas *Bewley* and Hugh *Stamper*, ſtanding at the Seſſions in *Carliſle* with their Hats on, were by the Juſtices committed to Priſon without any legal Cauſe aſſigned. After a Month's Confinement they were diſcharged without paying Fees : But Hugh *Stamper* was afterward arreſted for Fees, and again impriſoned and detained there one and twenty Weeks.

ANNO 1655. Matthew *Carpe* and Anthony *Fell* were impriſoned for appearing at Seſſions with their Hats on, and detained three Weeks. *Impriſonments for ſundry Cauſes.*

Matthew *Robinſon* and John *Dixon*, for refuſing to pay Tithes, were impriſoned at *Carliſle*, and afterward obliged to appear perſonally at *London*, above two Hundred and fifty Miles from their Habitations, to their great Expence and Trouble.

John *Peacock* and John *Stricket* Conſtables, refuſing to execute a Warrant of Diſtreſs for Tithes, were fined 1 *l.* 6 *s.* 8 *d.* and for Non-payment committed to Priſon.

Dorothy

GEORGE FOX, generally believed to have been the founder of the movement which came to be called the "Quakers", was born in 1624, at Leicester, the son of a shoemaker. Before he was out of his teens he left home and started his wanderings around the Midlands, reflecting on his beliefs and doubts. This was a time when many people were questioning established beliefs, and searching for alternatives. After all, this was at the beginning of the revolution which culminated in the large-scale rejection of the established Church, and of the Monarchy. The latter eventually lost its head literally, and the former, figuratively.

Eventually, in 1647, when he was 23, George Fox found enlightenment. 'The Lord opened unto me that being bred at Oxford or Cambridge was not enough to fit and qualify men to be ministers of Christ.' 'The Church was noe more holy than any other piece of grounde.' 'Every man was enlightened by the divine light of Christ.' This could be interpreted to mean that he believed that church-going was not all-important because God dwelled in men's and women's hearts.

As George Fox travelled, he discovered that many other thinking men had come to much the same conclusion, and he quickly found a nucleus of people who, with him, founded the Religious Society of Friends. This title however, came later, as did also a much more pacifist philosophy. In its early days the movement was much more radical and aggressive, and this aspect undoubtedly added to the fears and hatred felt by the establishment. The movement tended to attract mainly people from what we would describe today as the 'middle strata' of the population - merchants, shopkeepers, professional men, as well as many people whose search for beliefs had led them into the numerous other non-conformist sects at that time. Probably the nearest parallel to be found in modern times, was that crisis of conscience which arose in America during the 1960s and 1970s, at the time of the Vietnam War. Then too, many people felt estranged from established society, their estrangement manifesting itself in draft-evasion, mass-agitation, and in some cases, in joining a variety of quasi-religious sects.

This movement sprang up, along with many others, co-incident with the vacuum caused by the rejection, by Oliver Cromwell and his revolutionary followers, of the established Church. In Cumberland and Westmorland George Fox found ready adherants to his beliefs, and to quote from "Prelates and People of the Lake Counties" by C.M.L.Bouch, 'George Fox, in a few years was almost universally accepted as the sovereign pontiff of Cumberland.' Unlike many other sects which arose at that time, The Religious Society of Friends has survived down to today, undoubtedly thanks in part to the flexibility which it demonstrated within twenty years of its start.

After 1660, when the crown was restored to Charles II, persecution of the Quakers continued, as well as of other non- conformists, and only began to abate towards the end of the 1670s. The Toleration Act of 1689 was a big step forward in their acceptance, although even after that Quakers were prosecuted for their refusal to pay tithes to the Church of England. In the mid- seventeenth century men had been turned off their land for their Quaker beliefs. Later in the century their beliefs were put down to 'impulses of a warm brain', and a commentator, a doctor, recommended the 'discipline of a madhouse'. By the eighteenth century, reports Barry Reay in his "The Quakers and the English Revolution", 'Irish landlords were looking for Quaker tenants for their farms because they were careful husbandmen, and reliable with the rent.'

The Skelton family, of whom we shall hear more, as this story unfolds, and relationships with Huntingtons are revealed, had many Quaker connections. Manorial records for Holme Cultram noted that "on the other side of the parish, at Kirkbride and Angerton, there was a similar colony of Quakers, from about 1653" Their meeting house is mentioned by Quarter Sessions, April 9th 1698, "These are to certify that at the request of certaine people called Quakers, and by the presentment of the court pursuant to the late Act of Parliament, hath ordered one house at Kirkbride, lately built thereupon a certaine piece or parcel of ground by Arthur Skelton and other purchasers for that purpose to be recorded for a Meeting House for their religious worshipp."

Another Skelton involvement is recorded as follows: "One of the most notable of sufferers for the cause in its early days was Thomas Stordy of Moorhouse, a man of considerable property, and a descendant of Janet Skelton, great-niece of Abbott Chamber. In 1662 he went to visit friends in Carlisle gaol (the citadel), and was detained on suspicion. The oath of allegiance was tendered to him, and as he refused to swear at all, he was subjected to the penalty of premunire. The Sheriff sold up all his real and personal estate, and he was kept a prisoner for ten years, after which he was released, and his real estate was restored to him, at the intercession of the Earl of Carlisle. A few days later he was prosecuted for absenting himself from Church, and thrown into prison, where he died in December 1684". Thomas Stordy was by no means the only one to suffer in that corner of Cumberland; Joseph Besse's "Collection of the sufferings of the people called Quakers" mentions Hugh Stamper as having been imprisoned in Carlisle in 1655, and to references made in the ecclestiastical courts to presentments in 1670, of William Langcake, John Waite, and John Pearson, for failing to have their children baptised, and in 1675 references to a number of Skeltons, Sauls, and others for the same reasons. Besse's collection also reports,(Vol.1 pp 127, 128, 131,) that George Fox, in 1653, was imprisoned for seven weeks in Carlisle, sometimes among thieves and murderers, for 'preaching in the great worship house after the priest had ended his sermon, and for witnessing a good confession'.

The same report also records, among other punishments, that Robert Huntington was imprisoned for three months for preaching at Carlisle, and later, in 1655, was sentenced to imprisonment for twenty-two weeks for refusing to swear the Oath in Carlisle market. In 1670, as punishment for attending meetings at Burgh, Robert Huntington was fined, along with several others, a total of £90.14s.6d,(£90.72 ½pence, over £5000 in today's money) his share being taken up by the seizure of four cows and twenty-five sheep. These were later sold in the market, and the report notes that a succession of disasters befell their purchasers, one of them, Simon of Sowerby dying shortly afterwards, leaving the cows to his father, who also shortly died. Another purchaser, White of Caldbeck, who was persuaded by his wife to buy one of the cows, suffered the tragedy of losing his wife and child by drowning in a shallow pond.

The parish of Burgh-by-Sands had for several centuries been the home of some families of Huntingtons, and it is clear that they joined the new movement of Quakers in its very early days. The parish register for 1665 records the names of 13 persons who were 'presented' for non-conformism. It particularly cites Robert Huntington, and Rowland Huntington, because they "were the Churchwardens of Burgh, have no more to bee received".

When exactly Robert and Rowland became converted to the new movement, we do not know. Robert married Mary Martine in the church at Brigham, not far from Cockermouth, in 1653, and the probability is that both he and Rowland Huntington became converted to Quakerism shortly before they were 'expelled' as Churchwardens in Burgh in 1665. George Fox, who had devoted a lot of attention to Westmorland and Cumberland, made his last tour of Cumberland in 1664, when he held a big meeting at Pardsey Crag before returning south to Swarthmoor via Keswick and Rydal. Perhaps this meeting was the occasion when Robert and Rowland left the Church of England. It is obvious that they were men of religious commitment, being Churchwardens. Whether they lost their land as a punishment is not known, though many are known to have suffered that fate. As related above, the leading local Quaker, Thomas Stordy was imprisoned for a time in Carlisle, but it is fair to say that the Quakers of Cumberland were not so badly treated as were adherants from other parts of the country. Later, with the turn of the century, references to Quakers often contained a tone of ambivalent respect for them, "one of those who call themselves Quakers" was a frequent preamble to mention of them.

Robert and Mary Huntington, who lived at Boustead Hill, near Burgh had eight children, of which only one,Isaac, was a son. Mary, their first-born, married William Harrison in 1677, at Allonby. Margaret, born next, in 1657, died in infancy, and their third daughter, Elizabeth, born in 1658, only lived until 1681. The record of Elizabeth's burial in 1681 gives us a piece of additional information, because it says "daughter of Robert Huntington, a Minister." Women were just as frequently 'ministers' as were men among Friends. Robert's son Isaac, born in 1661, became a grocer in Carlisle, and married Ann Carlile at Burgh in 1677.

Robert and Mary's fourth daughter, Esther, born in 1664, did not marry until she was 35. Then,when she was living at Keswick, she married Thomas Laythes,of Dalehead, a wealthy and well-known Quaker. Thomas Laythes, (or Leathes as the family name subsequently became) had previously married, in 1651, Jane Bouch of Cockermouth, who owned considerable property at nearby Pardshaw. They had eight children between 1651 and 1669. In 1659 Thomas Laythes attended a Quaker meeting at Swarthmoor, became convinced of the truth of Quaker beliefs, and twice afterwards, in 1660 and 1664, was imprisoned for those beliefs. The Journal kept by George Fox records, "from Pardshaw Crag we went up into Westmorland, calling on the way upon Hugh Tickell, near Keswick, and upon Thomas Laythes, where friends came to visit us and we had a fine opportunity to be refreshed together."

Jane Laythes died in 1691, apparently not having been converted to the Quaker beliefs for she was buried in the quire at Crosthwaite Church. In 1699 Thomas married Esther Huntington at Pardshaw Crag, he being 71 years of age. Their marriage was short- lived, for Thomas died in 1701, and was buried in the Friends' burying place at Keswick. In the preface to the book printed after his death, of a collection of his published religious works, the following tribute to him was offered: "He was a man of an innocent life, and sweet temper of spirit: He loved peace with all men, and was careful to follow those things that made for his peace with the Lord;............Though a man of considerable estate, as to outward possessions, yet was he not lifted up thereby, but delighted to keep lowly in heart, which was an ornament to him, and made him honourable in his day."

We know nothing of Robert and Mary's fifth daughter, Abigail, born in 1669; it does not seem likely that she died in her childhood, for the Quakers were very punctilious with their record-keeping. Daughter number six, Anne, born in

1669, married John Newton in 1700, at Burgh, and of the last daughter, Deborah, born in 1672, as with Abigail, there is no further record. Maybe both Abigail and Deborah went to live outside the lakeland counties, as the Quakers seem to have been more than usually mobile, and the 'network' of the sect may have facilitated this.

Returning to Isaac and Ann, as was stated earlier they had a grocery business in Carlisle, and the births of their nine children were recorded at the Carlisle Meeting House. Their eldest son, named Isaac in 1686 became a Surgeon/Apothecary. He obviously went to live in Lincolnshire, where, at Gainsborough, a bachelor of 54 he died intestate. It was left to his grieving father, and his brother John, to take out Letters of Administration. The eldest daughter of Isaac and Ann, Elizabeth, was born in 1688, but no further record of her is to be found.

Next came John, born in 1691, and he followed his elder brother in vocation as an Apothecary. He, however remained in Carlisle, where he was admitted as a Freeman of the Carlisle Merchants Guild, on Low Sunday in 1717. John died in Carlisle in 1747 at the age of 56 and like his brother Isaac, a bachelor. His lengthy will revealed that materially his career had been successful, and it also revealed that he had remained a Quaker, for apart from some bequests of a few pounds to relatives, such as cousin Bridget Carlile, cousin George Moore, and cousin Mary Richardson, he left most of his property to 'Friends' Richard Waite, Elder of Newtown, and Thomas Mitchison of Carlisle.

The next of the offspring of Isaac and Ann, about which we know something other than date of birth, was Nathan, born in 1703. He followed his father in career and was a grocer in Carlisle until his early death in 1741, yet another bachelor. Possibly Quaker wives were difficult to come by, even after the turn of the century.

Because there were no further records of this branch, and because the three sons died bachelors, the Huntington name seems to have gone to the graves with them; neither do we have records of any marriages of the daughters, nor of the final son, Joseph, born in 1706. Possibly as has been indicated above, daughters may have moved out of Cumberland,married, and produced families elsewhere.

Rowland Huntington, is thought to have been Robert's brother, but he could equally likely have been Robert's cousin. A Robert Huntington had died in 1618 leaving bequests to Robert and Rowland Huntington; he is more likely to have been the grandfather of our two Quakers Robert and Rowland. Another Rowland Huntington of Boustead left a will in 1637, with a bequest to his son Robert, his wife Eleanor, and his daughter Dorothy. This indicates how difficult it can be, in the absence of any other evidence, to sort out relationships with accuracy.

Our Rowland, the Quaker, cousin or brother of Robert, married Katheron Robinson, at Burgh in 1674. This marriage was only a brief one, for Rowland died on 27th December 1681. Five children were born during this short period; John, in 1675, who died in infancy; Robert in 1676, who lived until 1741; Isaac, born in 1678; Elizabeth, born in 1679, who died in the following year; and Hanney (Hannah?), born on March 29th 1682, three months after her father's death. There are no records available of the events in the lives of Robert, Isaac, or of Hannah, and therefore, as with the descendants of Robert and Mary Huntington, the male line petered out before the mid-eighteenth century. Rowland's widow, Katherine, like Elizabeth, became a Minister; but it is not known whether, like Elizabeth she had travelled widely in the north of England and Scotland before her death in 1729. Probably though, after Rowland's death she did so.

It will particularly have been noticeable in this story of the two families in Burgh/by/Sands, how frequently death occurred in infancy or early childhood - at least six in those generations. This largely accounts for the belief that the 'life-span' in those days was considerably shorter than in current times. there were in fact lots of long lives, with people living to great ages just as some do today. To a large extent it was the numerous early deaths which actuarially reduced the life expectancy of a newly-born. By way of illustration, here is the record of the ages at death for a number of years, taken from the Parish Register of Burgh/by/Sands, whose recorder for the time being was good enough to find the time to note the information:

```
1799:   69,87,40,60,82,82,10 months,25
1800:   71,32,33,4,38,58,4,87,88,87,79,33,78,60,2mths
1801:   1,1,86,94,52,7weeks,36,56.
1802:   96,85,38,20,97,72,8,14,72,76,11.
```

This story has covered two families wherein all the members belonged to the Society of Friends, and it is incidentally noticeable that these families were in the middle strata of society at that time, neither Gentry nor Peasants, and it seems to have been this type of folk who were attracted to the Quaker persuasion. It is very likely that individual members of other Huntington families became converted; there were after all, very active centres of 'Quakerism' in several other places where Huntingtons lived, such as in the Cockermouth, Workington, Holme, Kirkbride, Wigton, Dalston localities, to say nothing of Carlisle. Despite a careful trawl (in many cases more than once) through virtually all of the Cumberland Parish Registers, recording the births, marriages and deaths of Huntingtons, there are numerous cases in which no further trace can be found. A lot of this can be attributed to loss of, or damage to, the original register documents, some to careless recording by the scribe at the time. But there is every chance that in respect of some, the record is absent because of a conversion to another religious sect, and Quakerism seems to have been the favourite alternative in Cumberland.

Reference was made earlier in this chapter to a Quaker network in the country as a whole. Because Quakers were persecuted for quite a period, and after this, often treated in less than a friendly spirit by those of a more conventional persuasion, it is not surprising that a high degree of cohesion was necessary to help them live within this unfriendly environment. They were not immigrant outsiders, like the Jews, or the Huegenots, who could settle in ghettoes, and live alongside one another; they were spread all over the country, and therefore had to rely on a network of mutual support, and mutual help, provided by their Meeting Houses, and with a good deal of social intercourse to bind them together.

A good example of this intercourse can be understood by reading a delightful booklet entitled "Excursion to Loweswater - a Lakeland Visit, 1865" by Mary Hodgson and Lydia Lunt. The book is beautifully illustrated in pen and ink, and in water colour. It is an account of an outing to the Lake District, at a time when travel was still a challenge, by a party of forty-four Quakers from

Manchester, who had been invited for a weekend at Waterend, Loweswater by
fellow-Quakers Robert and Rachel Jackson. The journey was not an easy one; by
train from Manchester to Windermere, from there by horse-drawn wagonette
north to Keswick; and south again to cross the Honister Pass for Loweswater, all
in pouring rain. The sketches reveal vividly how difficult and menacing was
Honister Pass in those days, and in clothes more appropriate, to contemporary
eyes, for an urban Sunday walk to Church! After a Sunday of leisure, which
included a picnic by the lovely Loweswater, and some religious observance, the
party set out at 4a.m. on the Monday morning for their return journey. Clearly
the outing was a great event, and in thanks to the Jacksons, Mary Hodgson and
Lydia Lunt wrote their acounts of the expedition in poetry and prose with the
beautiful illustrations, in a manner which even Arnold Bennett could not have
bettered. Most visitors to the Lake District are enchanted by its beauty, however
frequently they make the journey; the joy with which this party experienced their
visit, from their drab surroundings in Manchester, comes eloquently from the
pages of this book, and in today's jargon, it has to be voted as a "Good Read".

FRIENDS MEETING HOUSE, MO0RHOUSE, BUILT 1733
REPRODUCED BY COURTESY OF MR. DAVID M. BUTLER

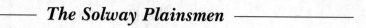

CHAPTER THREE

CHART NO.2
THE HUNTINGTON FAMILIES OF THURSBY
WESTWARD AND GREAT ORTON

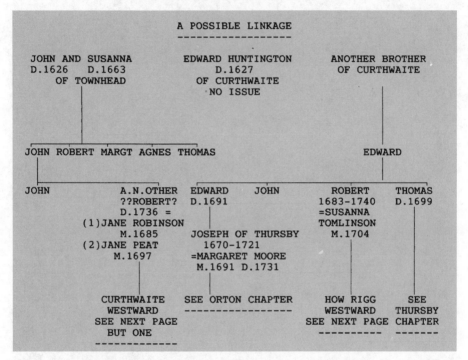

```
                      A POSSIBLE LINKAGE
                      -------------------

JOHN AND SUSANNA        EDWARD HUNTINGTON        ANOTHER BROTHER
D.1626    D.1663             D.1627              OF CURTHWAITE
  OF TOWNHEAD             OF CURTHWAITE
                          ·NO ISSUE



JOHN ROBERT MARGT AGNES THOMAS                       EDWARD


JOHN               A.N.OTHER   EDWARD     JOHN        ROBERT     THOMAS
                   ??ROBERT?   D.1691               1683-1740    D.1699
                   D.1736 =                         =SUSANNA
                   (1)JANE ROBINSON                 TOMLINSON
                      M.1685                         M.1704
                   (2)JANE PEAT   JOSEPH OF THURSBY
                      M.1697        1670-1721
                                  =MARGARET MOORE
                                  M.1691 D.1731


                   CURTHWAITE  SEE ORTON CHAPTER    HOW RIGG      SEE
                   WESTWARD    -----------------    WESTWARD    THURSBY
                   SEE NEXT PAGE                    SEE NEXT PAGE CHAPTER
                   BUT ONE                          ----------   -------
                   -------------
```

I t must be emphasised that the Family Tree projected above is entirely speculative. (Unlike those on the next two pages, which have been built up from references in Parish Registers, copies of wills and from census returns). The recording of events, that is the baptisms, marriages and deaths, in respect of the inhabitants of Westward, Thursby, and Wigton, is to be found in any one of the above parish registers, plus that of Dalston, and this seems to be irrespective of the parish to which they belonged. Probably this overlapping occurred because the Huntingtons in those parishes were really one big family group, whose common ancestors were only a generation or so back in time. A number of wills are available to help piece together the pattern of relationships in the period for which no other records exist. Unfortunately though, first names such as John, Robert, Edward, Joseph and William, were used so regularly, that it would be a miracle for the speculative tree to be exactly right. A few clues have helped ; we have seen from the Percy Survey of the district in 1589, that one branch held land on lease at How Rigg, in Curthwaite, passed on from generation to generation. Fortunately that helped to distinguish between the two families described below.

CHART NO.3
THE DESCENDANTS OF ROBERT & SUSANNA HUNTINGTON

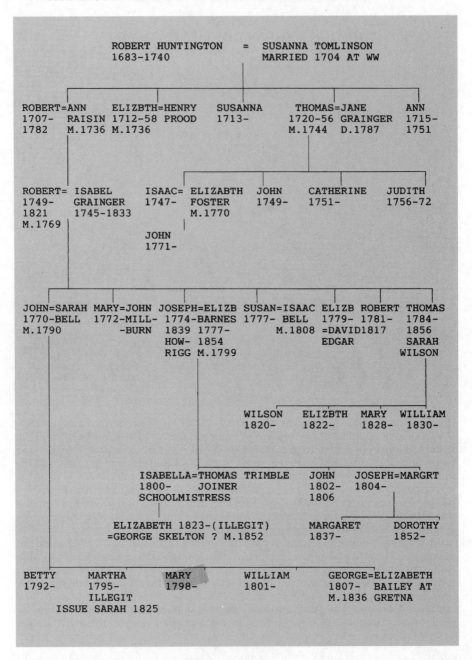

ROBERT HUNTINGTON   =   SUSANNA TOMLINSON
1683-1740   MARRIED 1704 AT WW

ROBERT=ANN   ELIZBTH=HENRY   SUSANNA   THOMAS=JANE   ANN
1707- RAISIN   1712-58 PROOD   1713-   1720-56 GRAINGER   1715-
1782   M.1736   M.1736   M.1744 D.1787   1751

ROBERT= ISABEL   ISAAC= ELIZABTH JOHN   CATHERINE   JUDITH
1749-   GRAINGER   1747- FOSTER   1749-   1751-   1756-72
1821   1745-1833   M.1770
M.1769

                    JOHN
                    1771-

JOHN=SARAH MARY=JOHN JOSEPH=ELIZB SUSAN=ISAAC ELIZB ROBERT THOMAS
1770-BELL 1772-MILL- 1774-BARNES 1777- BELL 1779- 1781- 1784-
M.1790   -BURN 1839 1777-   M.1808   =DAVID1817 1856
                 HOW- 1854   EDGAR   SARAH
                 RIGG M.1799   WILSON

                            WILSON   ELIZBTH   MARY   WILLIAM
                            1820-   1822-   1828-   1830-

                    ISABELLA=THOMAS TRIMBLE JOHN   JOSEPH=MARGRT
                    1800-   JOINER   1802-   1804-
                    SCHOOLMISTRESS   1806

                 ELIZABETH 1823-(ILLEGIT)   MARGARET   DOROTHY
                 =GEORGE SKELTON ? M.1852   1837-   1852-

BETTY   MARTHA   MARY   WILLIAM   GEORGE=ELIZABETH
1792-   1795-   1798-   1801-   1807- BAILEY AT
          ILLEGIT   M.1836 GRETNA
     ISSUE SARAH 1825

CHART NO.4
THE DESCENDANTS OF ROBERT AND
JANE HUNTINGTON OF WESTWARD

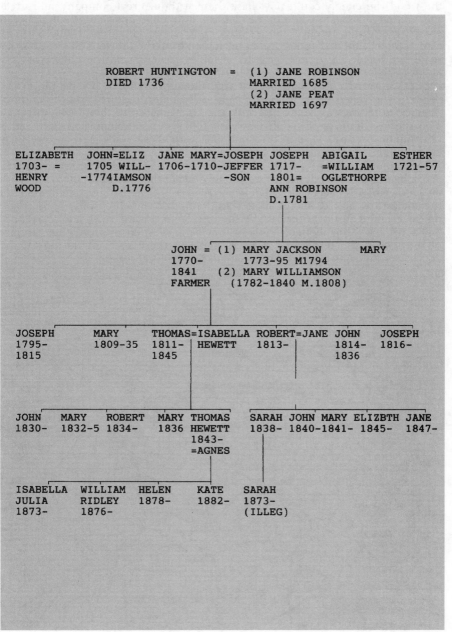

```
        ROBERT HUNTINGTON   =   (1) JANE ROBINSON
        DIED 1736               MARRIED 1685
                                (2) JANE PEAT
                                MARRIED 1697


ELIZABETH  JOHN=ELIZ  JANE MARY=JOSEPH  JOSEPH  ABIGAIL    ESTHER
1703-  =   1705 WILL- 1706-1710-JEFFER  1717-   =WILLIAM    1721-57
HENRY      -1774IAMSON           -SON   1801=   OGLETHORPE
WOOD            D.1776                   ANN ROBINSON
                                        D.1781


                    JOHN = (1) MARY JACKSON        MARY
                    1770-      1773-95 M1794
                    1841   (2) MARY WILLIAMSON
                    FARMER     (1782-1840 M.1808)


JOSEPH       MARY      THOMAS=ISABELLA ROBERT=JANE  JOHN    JOSEPH
1795-        1809-35   1811-  HEWETT   1813-        1814-   1816-
1815                   1845                         1836


JOHN   MARY    ROBERT  MARY  THOMAS       SARAH JOHN  MARY ELIZBTH JANE
1830-  1832-5  1834-   1836  HEWETT       1838- 1840-1841- 1845-  1847-
                             1843-
                             =AGNES


ISABELLA  WILLIAM   HELEN    KATE   SARAH
JULIA     RIDLEY    1878-    1882-  1873-
1873-     1876-                     (ILLEG)
```

Westward Forest, according to evidence given in 1569 before a commission of enquiry into enclosures, had been: "so thick of wood as poor men used in all dangerous times to drive their cattle into the said forest, and when they were in the wood the enemy could not chase them without great company, and great time to do it, by means whereof the country always had knowledge and gathered company to the rescue." So relates 'The Lake Counties 1500-1830' by C.M.L.Bouch, and G.P.Jones. As has been seen from the previous chapter, border strife had formed a permanent part of life for several centuries, and was only about to abate at the end of the sixteenth century.

The Westward Forest had been a vital life support for many people in the district, who relied upon it for the right of common pasture, and the enquiry mentioned above was concerned with the land enclosures then being effected. The interests of the poor people who wished to retain, undiminished, their rights of common pasture, were in direct conflict with those wishing to enclose their land.

The enquiry, reporting in 1572, revealed that 127 enclosures, involving 545 acres, had been effected, which presumably meant that 127 new tenements, with an average of 4 1/4 acres each, had been created. Houses had been built on 32 of the enclosures, and 205 acres allotted to them, that is each of these houses had, on the average, just over 6 acres. Of the rest, 95 enclosures, with a total of about 340 acres, had been allotted to tenants having ancient farmsteads. Thus, in spite of the loss of the traditional pasture rights in those parts of the forest, the enclosures did constitute an improvement for the local society.

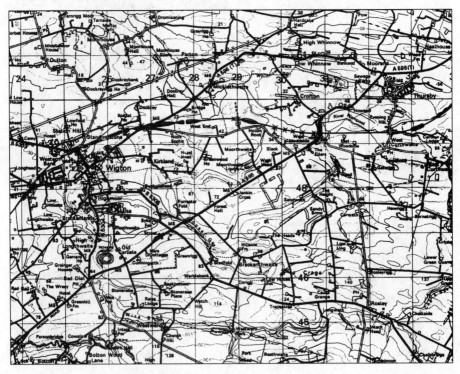

We can guess too that the local Huntington families were the beneficiaries of this early trend toward land enclosures. Almost certainly at that time they could be categorised as 'tenants having ancient farmsteads', henceforth entitled to enclose their land and to build homes on it, rather than having to live in the village, and travel possibly some miles each day to work it.

The Percy Survey of 1578 recorded several Huntington land tenancies at Thursby and Westward as follows:

"At How Ridge, with East Curthwaite, John Huntington the Eldest holdeth one close containing 7 acres, lately improved and renteth by the year 2/8d."

"Thomas Huntington holdeth at How Ridge a tenement, a barn, a sheep house, and one close, lately improved, containing 2 acres, and renteth by the year 12d."

"John Huntington the Elder holdeth at How Ridge, a tenement, a barn, and other buildings, and one close, lately improved, containing 5_ acres, and renteth by the year 2/8d."

"John Huntington the younger holdeth in the How Ridge, one close, lately improved, containing three acres, and renteth by the year 16d".

"William Huntington holdeth in the How Ridge, one close, lately improved, containing three acres, and renteth by the year 16d."

"John Huntington the son of Lawrence, of West Curthwaite, holdeth one oven house, and half an acre of land, rented at 2d, and also one close containing 1 rood rented at 2d., and in the How Ridge, three acres rented by the year 16d."

The oldest will of which we have a copy is that of John Huntington, of Thursby, dated 1574, bequeathing his property to his son John, (presumably "the younger" mentioned in the 1578 Percy Survey), and a later will by Margaret Huntington of Westward, in 1580, makes bequests to "John my stepson, Jane my stepdaughter, my stepson's three children, Robert, Edward and Janet, My stepson John's wife Dorothy, Thomas and Edward Huntington,..........." Clearly, those small strips of land listed in the Percy Survey were to be still further divided up, or some of the descendants would have to find an alternative living.

It is interesting, before moving on in time, to note also the Calendar of Border Papers, 1560-94, for this district. Border raids were to continue to be a problem to Cumbrians until the reign of the Stuart Monarchs at the beginning of the 17th century and, to some degree, even after that. The Wardens of each sector of the Borders were responsible for maintaining the availability of a civilian militia, to be able to respond to any incursions by the Grahams, the Armstrongs, and other marauding families from across the border and the Firth. Thus the Calendar recorded the names of those available, with weapons, for call-out in case of need. These included:

"Westwarde: Thomas Huntington, Lance, John Huntington, Bow,Arrows

"East Curthwaite: William Huntington, Spear, Joseph Huntington, Spear, Edward Huntington, Bow, Arrows.

"Burgh-by-Sands: Theire is foure surnames theire; Liddalles, Glasters, Huntingtons and Hodgsons, but theire is not many of none of them." (sic!)

The parish of Westward is about 4_ miles in length and breadth, and is bounded on the north by Thursby, on the east by Dalston and Sebergham, on the south by Caldbeck and Bolton, and on the west by Wigton. The parish Church stands on Church Hill, as does a school, endowed in 1754 by John Jefferson. The parish is a large one in area, and the church is tucked away in the south-east corner of it, which undoubtedly explains why many of the inhabitants frequently used Thursby, Dalston and Wigton churches for convenience, if they happened to be nearer. The parish also contains Old Carlisle, the site and remains of a Roman station. This is one of the most fertile districts on the Solway Plain.

It is interesting to note that the 1829 Parish Directory lists among its farming community, within the Woodside 'township':

John Huntington, of East Curthwaite, Yeoman, and

Joseph Huntington, of Howrigg, Farmer.

So the family land holding at How Ridge (Howrigg) had been handed down through the generations, between 1578, (probably much earlier than that) and the date of the Directory, 1829. Today it is a prosperous looking farm still, but no longer in the family.

HOWRIGG FARM, CURTHWAITE, 1993. SITE OF HUNTINGTON LANDHOLDINGS FROM 1579, (PROBABLY EARLIER), UNTIL THE MID-EIGHTEENTH CENTURY.

From the surviving parish registers, (having to jump about from one parish record to another), the earliest being in the late seventeenth century, we pick up the two 'Westward' families, both of them, at the turn of the century being headed by Roberts, whom we think to have been cousins.(see the first page of this chapter 'a possible linkage')

The elder of these two Roberts was married to Susanna Tomlinson, who must have been a local girl, close to the family, because she was named as a god-daughter to Thomas Huntington of Moorthwaite, in his 1733 will. Robert and Susanna lived at Howrigg, and they had five children, including two sons, Robert and Thomas. Their elder son Robert, who was to inherit the land in 1740, married Ann Raisin a few years beforehand. He lived for 75 years before handing it on to their only son, also named Robert. The latter had married Isabel Grainger, and both of them lived to good ages of 72 and 88 respectively. They produced a good crop of children, seven in total, all surviving the hazards of infancy and youth.

Unusually, their eldest son John, born in 1770, did not take on his parents' land, but instead was a weaver. It is presumed that he became a weaver for his livelihood during his long wait to inherit the land. In the event, when Robert finally died in 1821, he provided quite handsomely for his wife Isabella, and for all his children. He left £100 each to his wife and his sons, and his daughters Susan and Elizabeth, and an annuity to his daughter Mary. He had two properties to dispose of, one at East Curthwaite which went to John, and the other at West Curthwaite (Howrigg) which went to Joseph.

John, the heir at law, either decided that inheriting the farm land at the age of 51 was not a good prospect, or that he did not fancy himself as a farmer,and stuck to his loom. Married to Sarah Bell in 1790, he fathered three daughters before becoming the father of two sons, William and George, his address being given as 'Foggythwaite'. George eloped, with Elizabeth Bailey, of Hesket-in-the-forest, in 1836, to Gretna Green. Certainly George was not under age to marry, he was 29. So maybe Elizabeth was under age, or perhaps they did it for the romance.

It was Joseph the next son, who became the Farmer. But he also had a wait before that happened, for the same reason as his elder brother. In the meantime he became a joiner, and at other times he described his occupation as 'Cowper' (Cooper). In due course he moved into Howrigg, with his wife Elizabeth (Betty) nee Barnes whom he had married when he was 25, and she,22. These young ages of marriage were a sign of the comparative prosperity into which he and his siblings had been born - despite the poor economy at that time, post, the Napoleonic wars. Joseph and Elizabeth had only three children, (another sign of prosperity?) Isabella, born in 1800, John, born in 1802, and destined to live less than three years, and Joseph, born in 1804.

In 1823 Isabella had an illegitimate daughter, Elizabeth, who was baptised at Thursby. She became a schoolmistress at nearby Dalston, and later, in 1841, she married Thomas Trimble, at the age of 41, at Dalston. Perhaps all was not well in the Trimble household, for Isabella's mother, Elizabeth Huntington, in her 1854 will left £250 to 'her good friend and neighbour' John Twentyman, Yeoman, of Brocklebank, on trust to invest, the interest to be paid to daughter Isabella Trimble. She thus prevented the money from coming into the possession of Thomas Trimble. In the event of Isabella's death the money was to be divided equally between her illegitimate daughter, Elizabeth, and her legitimate son, Joseph Trimble. She left her son Joseph Huntington £250. He turns up in the

1883 census, aged 77, his occupation given as Husbandman, with his wife Margaret, aged 71, occupation given as Labourer's wife, and one of their two daughters, Margaret, aged 43, unmarried. Their address in Dalston was 'Old School' Dalston. Had this been mother Isabella's school? Dorothy, the younger of their daughters was not listed; perhaps she had married. Isabella's illegitimate daughter, Elizabeth married George Skelton in 1852.

Of the four younger siblings of Joseph and Elizabeth Huntington, Susan married Isaac Bell in 1808, (brother to Sarah, John's wife?); Elizabeth married David Edgar; Robert died when he was 36, and the youngest, Thomas, married Sarah Wilson, becoming an Ironmonger in Carlisle. They had four children, Wilson, Elizabeth Mary, and William. It was about this time that the practice of naming a child with the mother's maiden name became popular.

We are not told who took on the family land at Howrigg after Joseph Huntington's tenure. Possibly his widow, Elizabeth did for a time; she seemed to know her mind; but at her death she was living at Chalkfoot in the east of the parish, not at Howrigg. We can be certain that her youngest and only surviving son did not take it on because he described himself as a Husbandman/Labourer, not as a farmer. We know that Thomas, the younger brother of Joseph and Elizabeth did not inherit; he was the ironmonger. The presumption has to be that, there being no male Huntington heir, Elizabeth sold the property, and ended up 'cash-rich' by the standards of those times. Her husband, Joseph, had died in 1839, and if she did 'sell up' at that time, she was blessed with good luck or prescience. Those were hard times to be in the farming business. Farm prices had risen steeply, and stayed high, during the Napoleonic Wars, but had plummetted with the wars's end. To this was added the impact on farming prosperity of the Corn Laws. An example of the trend is given by the record of the annual average price of wheat as follows:

1817	96s 11d per quarter
1818	86s 3d " "
1819	74s. 6d " "
1820	67s 10d " "
1821	56s 1d " "
1822	44s 7d " "

The situation remained grim for farmers until eventually the Corn Law was repealed in the mid-1840s, with the result that a lot of farmers left the business, and they and their labourers too, joined the trek to the cities and towns, to become industrial workers. It has been estimated that between 1770 and 1820, the number of 'statesmen' with their own land was halved. The land was taken up by wealthier men who could afford and justify the cost of equipment, which would make farming more productive. In spite of this trend, the small farmers in Cumberland were more resilient and tenacious than in many other parts of the country, and more of them clung on to weather the difficulties.

The other Robert Huntington of Westward lived in East Curthwaite, was a farmer, and he married twice. His first wife died shortly after their marriage, and he married Jane Peat in 1697. All of the children listed on the tree are of the second marriage.

Robert and Jane had two sons and four daughters, and we know that they all survived to adulthood. Both sons, John and Joseph stayed in agriculture as Yeomen. John's will of 1774 left all to his wife Betty, including his 'stock of horses and cattle', together with the crop of hay, corn, and grain, (the will was made in August), plus the sum of eighty pounds, with bequests to his maid- servant, Susan Reed, £20, to his nephew Robert Huntington a chest, a dresser, a closet and a cupboard, "on condition that he permits his sisters Jane and Abigail to continue to live in his house where they were living, or else to find them alternative accommodation". Having no children of his own, John nominated his brothers and sisters as heirs in the event that Betty died before him.

However Betty did outlive him, but only by a couple of years, dying in June 1776. She also left a will, leaving small bequests to nephews and nieces on her side of the family, and £10 (about £500 in today's money)to the maid-servant Susan Reed, The main part of her estate was left to her nephews George Williamson, and her brother George Williamson, Clerk (in holy orders). These two were also nominated as executors. From words used in her late husband's will, of which she had been the main beneficiary, it can be inferred that Betty had brought part of their assets to the marriage. An interesting and common device was used in drafting her will. In order to prevent the challenging, by any other relative, of the provisions of her will, after her death, she left a nominal sum, one pound, one shilling to her brother-in- law. He could not then afterwards assert that he had been overlooked and try to overturn the will. Finally she gained immortality by bequeathing £10 (about £500 in 1995 money) to be distributed to the poor of Westward and Thursby. Her brother-in- law, Joseph and his wife, took over the task of perpetuating their family's line, but only by a narrow margin of one son, John, born in 1770. John described himself as a farmer, and in the 1829 Directory, he was described as a Yeoman living at East Curthwaite. He firstly married Mary Jackson of Thursby in April 1794, by licence, but she died in May of the following year, aged 23, a couple of days after giving birth to a son, Joseph. He however was destined to live only 20 years, dying in 1815.

John did not marry again until 1808, when he and Mary Williamson were married on Christmas Eve, at Thursby. Possibly Mary was a niece or great niece, of John's aunt, Betty Huntington (nee Williamson). It was probably a 'shot-gun' wedding, because their daughter Mary was baptised on 16th July 1809. This unfortunate child was also to have a short life, as she died in 1835, aged only 25. Their next child, Thomas, born in 1811 also only lived a brief 34 years, dying in 1845. But he managed to fit in a marriage, and the siring of five children by his wife Isabella Hewitt, whom he married at Dalston in May 1830. Their first son, John arrived in October, and their second son, child number five, was baptised Thomas Hewett in 1843.

John and Mary's fourth child, Robert, born in 1813, married a Jane, maiden-name unknown, and they had a family of five, four of them daughters, the first one being Sarah, born in 1838. The only one of this family recorded in the 1881 Cumberland Census was Sarah, aged 42, unmarried, described as a housekeeper to a farmer at Wythop, and accompanied by a daughter, also Sarah and aged 8.Reverting to Thomas Hewett, the youngest of Thomas and Isabella's family, we know that he married Agnes, a lady from Glasgow. They figured in the Maryport Census of 1881, Thomas as a Foreman at the Gasworks, living at Lena Works House. Their four children, (up to that date) were aged from 8 years down to 1 year. So, with the death in 1845 of Thomas Huntington, Husbandman, there appears to have ended, for that branch of the Huntingtons anyway, a dependence on agriculture for a living. The better opportunities offered by industry, and the greater mobility available, proved to be a magnet. In the second half of the nineteenth century, it was to be left to only a few Huntingtons to be involved with farming, notably, as we shall see later on, in the Eden Valley.

ST. HILDA'S CHURCH, WESTWARD.
PHOTO BY KINDNESS OF WILSON SWAN.

It will have been noted that, particularly with the foregoing branches of the family, many members are not accounted for. This is because no mention of them was found during a detailed search of parish registers, census records, or wills and other documents We do know that many registers were incomplete; some were badly preserved and became illegible, some were destroyed, and some events simply were not recorded for one reason or another. Furthermore the research conducted was confined to Cumberland and Westmorland which alone required a vast amount of time. Of course, given a lifetime devoted solely to this research, it could have been possible to search through all registers and census records, for the whole of Britain, any spare time being spent researching records also in North America, and Australasia. The haystack is unfortunately too big! Therefore the writer has to be content, in the course of this book, to confine his enquiry to Cumbrian records only, and to hope that some of its readers will recognise strands of their ancestry, and perhaps will be able add to the knowledge offered herein. Good fortune has provided the writer with many valuable helpers and advisors. One of these advisors, when a particular puzzle has obstructed the progress of research, has frequently pointed out how necessary it is to leave some of the discoveries to later generations. What a wise person! I take her advice, and hope that the trail which follows in the ensuing chapters will indeed stimulate others to make a much more complete job than this. Any who do make the attempt can be guaranteed a thrilling and satisfying task.

BELOW: MOOREND, THURSBY. BELIEVED TO HAVE BEEN THE HOME OF THOMAS (1663-1713) AND MARY HUNTINGTON.

CHAPTER FOUR

CHART NO.5
THE HUNTINGTONS OF GREAT ORTON, CUMBRIA

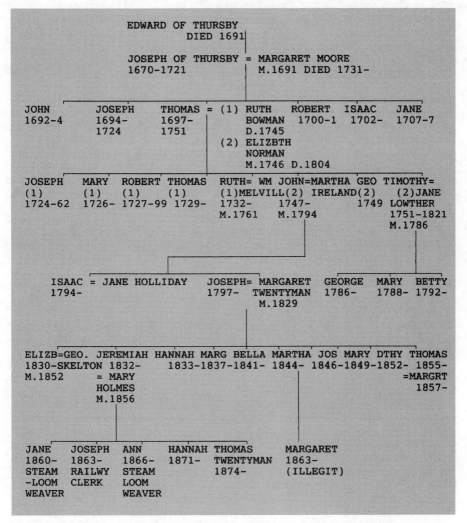

```
                    EDWARD OF THURSBY
                        DIED 1691

                JOSEPH OF THURSBY = MARGARET MOORE
                    1670-1721       M.1691 DIED 1731-

JOHN      JOSEPH    THOMAS = (1) RUTH    ROBERT  ISAAC   JANE
1692-4    1694-     1697-       BOWMAN   1700-1  1702-   1707-7
          1724      1751        D.1745
                            (2) ELIZBTH
                                NORMAN
                                M.1746 D.1804

JOSEPH   MARY   ROBERT THOMAS  RUTH= WM  JOHN=MARTHA GEO  TIMOTHY=
(1)      (1)    (1)    (1)     (1)MELVILL(2) IRELAND(2) 1749 (2)JANE
1724-62  1726-  1727-99 1729-  1732-      1747-          LOWTHER
                               M.1761     M.1794         1751-1821
                                                         M.1786

        ISAAC = JANE HOLLIDAY   JOSEPH= MARGARET   GEORGE  MARY  BETTY
        1794-                   1797-  TWENTYMAN   1786-   1788- 1792-
                                       M.1829

ELIZB=GEO. JEREMIAH HANNAH MARG BELLA MARTHA JOS MARY DTHY THOMAS
1830-SKELTON 1832-  1833-1837-1841- 1844- 1846-1849-1852- 1855-
M.1852     = MARY                                          =MARGRT
           HOLMES                                          1857-
           M.1856

JANE    JOSEPH   ANN    HANNAH THOMAS     MARGARET
1860-   1863-    1866-  1871-  TWENTYMAN  1863-
STEAM   RAILWY   STEAM         1874-      (ILLEGIT)
-LOOM   CLERK    LOOM
WEAVER           WEAVER
```

Of Great Orton's school, William Hutchinson's "History of Cumberland", published in 1797, tells us that one Thomas Pattinson, a bachelor and parishioner, bequeathed £100 for an endowment in 1785. The History continues: "The present schoolmaster and parish clerk, Richard Dixon, has taught in the said school for forty years, and consequently has been the instructor of most of the present inhabitants. He calls himself Happy Dick and is generally so styled by the parishioners." The village of Great Orton, or Overton," being so named in respect of the situation and higher standing of that place in reference to its surroundings". The history related that, from a place called Parson's Thorn, close to the village, fifteen parish churches may be clearly seen, besides several in Scotland, with a beautiful view of Gretna. It stated that several towns may be seen, namely the city of Carlisle, the market towns of Brampton, Wigton, and Longtown; likewise Penrith Beacon, Cross-fell, the 'Scotch' mountains, and a number of other prominent heights.

The parish is bounded on the east by the parish of St. Mary, Carlisle, by Burgh to the north, by Kirkbampton and Aikton to the west, and by Thursby and Dalston to the south. Like its neighbours the village lay in the path of the moss-troopers from across the Solway Firth. In earlier times there was a large fosse or ditch just north of the village, where an iron chain, which was locked each night, went across the road. It was called Barras Gate. Not far to the west of there is a place still called 'Watchtree', "whence any raid could be detected afar by the sounds of clashing churchbells, or the bleating and lowing of driven stock, or perhaps the more dread sight of flaming stacks against the darkness of the midnight sky." There is a tradition that "one of these moss-troopers being observed, a villager named John Wilson, shot at him with an arrow from a distance of 400 yards, piercing the invader's thigh, and pinning him to his saddle". There is every possibility that the range of this shot increased with the telling of the tale over the years! Nevertheless, the historian's vivid words convey very clearly to us, across the centuries, the horror and fear which were nightly companions of the people living on the Solway Plain, especially on dark winter nights.

In those early times the village must have been fairly important, because in 1732 there were 81 families;8 Quakers,3 Presbyterians in 1750, 82 houses, and in 1791, the population was 372," all Church of England except 10 Quakers". The same historian tells us that there were, unfortunately, no house ruins left to show us how much larger Orton once was, as the houses being "clay daubins" were carted away as excellent manure as soon as they fell into ruin. "Certain families occupy the principle places in the Orton registers; their names are, (1) Twentyman, (2) Moore (3) Norman, (4) Nixon, (5) Wilson, (6) Hind, (7) Blaine, (8) Johnston, (9) Pattinson or Pattyson." As will be seen from the Great Orton registers, Huntingtons married into the Twentyman, Moore, Norman and Blayne families.

Occasionally we come across an especially informative chronicler such as this, and he continued, "In 1596/7, an attack of some pestilence (believed nowadays to have been Typhus accompanying famine conditions) seems to have devastated Orton terribly. In these two years as many as 54 deaths are recorded". "In 1668 we find Joseph, son of John XXman of Woodhouses buried, being the first corpse buried in woollen at Orton Church, according to (the) act in the case made and providing" (An act of parliament ordered it, to encourage the woollen trade, and there was a fine for burying people in anything else. Mention of it in the parish register was made only because it was the first instance of compliance at Great Orton. Subsequently it was taken for granted.

Imagine comparable legislation today, ruling that coffins should be of 're-cycled cardboard, or other environmentally friendly, organic materials'!) Another interesting entry to which the historian draws our attention for 1783 was, "The duty on baptisms, marriages and burials took place October 2nd 1785". The duty was not in fact on baptisms, but on the registration of them, and was 3d per entry in the parish registers. It was a very unfair and unpopular tax, leading to failure by the vicars to register, out of consideration for the poorer parishioners. The act was repealed in 1794.

Another entry in the register, a baptism in May 1678, which caught the chronicler's eye and then his imagination, "Ann, illegitimate and supposed daughter of a young man who is gone away amongst the volunteers, and of Lucy Johnson of Little Orton, spinster". The historian asks, "Who were these volunteers, and what army was there to repel?" The answer lay in the sudden invitation to England of the Prince of Orange, and his wedding to Mary, the eldest daughter of the Duke of York,(later James II 1685-88) and the presumptive heiress to the throne. As this would lead to a protestant dynasty, the army was mobilised by those of catholic faith. An opposing protestant army was raised by Parliament, and no doubt Lucy's young man followed the common practice of joining the army in order to avoid his parental responsibilities.

Right from their earliest settlement in Cumberland, Huntingtons must have been familiar with Great Orton, those from Burgh passing through it on their way south, although none of that name was recorded as from the village in the Calendar of Border Papers

BELOW:ST. GILES' CHURCH, GREAT ORTON.
REPRODUCED BY KINDNESS OF MR. WILSON SWAN .

We have a copy of a will, dated 1593, of 'Thomas Huntington of Orton', but he is believed to have belonged to a Thursby branch, the reference to Orton being because he had been a priest, probably an assistant curate at the church of St.Giles Great Orton. Another will, dated 1599, was by David Huntington of Orton who left bequests to "my oldest son John, my daughter Annas, and my son Rowland" The inventory attached to his will valued his belongings at £7.19s.6d (£7- 97 ½ pence, about £400 in today's money). It is thought, though, that he had led a peripatetic life, for although his daughter Annas was married to Robert Blayne, at St.Giles' in 1617, his sons John and Rowland were married at Wigton, the former to Elizabeth Clerk in 1616, and the latter in 1607 to Ellis (Alice?) Vaux. David Huntington's will directed that he should be buried'within the church of Bownes' (Bowness).

A branch of the Huntington family was established at Great Orton on the marriage of Joseph Huntington of Thursby (1670-1721) to Margaret Moore, in 1691, at Great Orton. An earlier connection with the Moores had been made in 1685 by the marriage of John Moore (Junior) to Jane Huntington. Joseph was a son of Edward Huntington of Thursby, who died in 1691.

The family home was referred to as 'Mainsfold', and six children were born there, of which only three survived infancy; two of these barely making manhood before dying, leaving only Thomas Huntington (1697-1751) to perpetuate that branch.

Thomas did his duty as perpetuator conscientiously. His 1751 will described him as a Yeoman. His father, Joseph, had died in 1721, and his mother, Margaret, in 1731, at which time he inherited the estate. Joseph's will had bequeathed to his eldest son, Joseph, (then still alive, he died in 1724) a bedstead, a table, a dresser, a gang of cart-gear, a great chest in the bower, two bushels of Bigg (barley), three bushels of oats, with ploughs and plough- gear; to his youngest son Isaac (then also still alive) he left £10; to Joseph, his brother's son, a brown-backed 'heiffer'; to his wife Margaret, the rest of his personal estate, goods and chattels; his second son Thomas was appointed executor but received no bequest. However, by the time of his mother's death in 1731, he appears to have been the only survivor, and duly took out Letters of Administration.

Thomas Huntington married twice, the first time, in 1723 to Ruth Bowman, by whom he had five children. Ruth Huntington died in 1745, and in the following year he married Elizabeth Norman of Great Orton, and they had three sons, John, George and Timothy. Shortly afterwards, Thomas died, in 1751.

His will bequeathed, to his eldest son and heir-apparent, Joseph, and, Thomas Furness, of Little Orton, (? a son-in-law ?), all and each and every one of his freehold messuages, lands, tenements and hereditaments with every one of their appurtenances, situate lying and being at Orton; he willed that certain properties should be disposed of after his death, in order to make provision for his wife, and their other children, with the exception of his son Robert, whom he specifically declared, should receive nothing. Whatever sin or sins, Robert had committed, we are not told. Obviously Thomas had given a lot of thought to the disposal of his estate, and equally obviously this was not insubstantial because he additionally willed that Joseph, the executor, should have £75 for his trouble. This sum alone was quite handsome, and related to today's values, was the equivalent of nearly £4000.

Joseph remained a bachelor, and died intestate in 1762, at the age of 32,only eleven years after his father had died, and his older brother Robert (the blacksheep?) took out letters of Administration. In 1799 Robert died, presumably also never having married, and he left his belongings to his stepmother Elizabeth Huntington, his sister Ruth, who had married William Melvill, and his half-brothers, John and Timothy.

Elizabeth Huntington outlived her husband Thomas by 53 years, and she evidently outlived her expectations by 26 years, because she made her will in 1778, but lived until June 1804. In her will she bequeathed "to my daughter in law Jane, the wife of my son Timothy, all my messuages, tenements, houses, outhouses, lands, hereditaments and premises with the appurtenances situate at Great Orton or elsewhere (author's note, the lawyers must have been paid by the word), except as hereinafter mentioned......... and immediately after the death of the said Jane, I give and devise the same to Mary, the daughter of my son Timothy. In case Mary should die before her mother, and without leaving issue, then I give and devise the same to my said son Timothy and to his heirs. I give and bequeath to my son Timothy all that dwelling house and shop now in his occupation, as also my bier, calf-house and Dunghill stead thereunto adjoining, together with my parcel of common ground containing about eight acres, situate at Mosscrook in the parish of Orton. But nevertheless I order and direct that the said Jane Huntington shall be at liberty to at least four cartloads of turves yearly during her natural life, and out of the said parcel of common land shall also have during such time the use of one half of the said dunghill stead. I give and bequeath to my son John the sum of six pounds............... I give to my said granddaughter Mary Huntington, all my household furniture and wearing apparel. All the residue of my money, securities for money, goods chattels and credits I bequeath to my said son Timothy, charged with the payment of my debts, legacies, and funeral expenses, and I appoint him as Executor............"

An interesting will, and one wonders why Timothy's mother so carefully stipulated that her daughter-in-law should have a lot of her estate left to her, in preference to her own son. Perhaps she did not consider him responsible enough, and wished to ensure that her granddaughter Mary should have an inheritance. It is interesting to note that Timothy died intestate in 1821, and that his widow Jane had to apply for Letters of Administration. Though he lived until he was seventy he had not taken the trouble to make a will. Jane's letters of administration offered one piece of information not previously known to us; that Timothy Huntington was a shoemaker by trade; hence the shop left him in his mother's will. She must have backed his enterprise.

Unfortunately, current maps of Cumbria do not shew "Mainsfold" in Great Orton, and it must have been demolished, or have suffered destruction by fire. It seems to have been a farm, which had provided the earlier Huntingtons with a good living. These were the times when lands were being enclosed, and possibly Timothy saw " the writing on the wall", (quite literally), and took to his last.

Timothy's older brother, John married late. Born in 1747, he married Martha Ireland at Dalston in August 1794. This did not hinder his fecundity though, for Martha presented him with Isaac in October 1794; a shot-gun wedding, supposedly supervised by Mr. Ireland. John and Martha produced another son, Joseph in 1797, before calling it a day. Isaac married Jane Holliday at Great Orton in 1832, but no issue were recorded in Cumbrian parish registers. As is so often the case though, his brother Joseph, who married Margaret Twentyman at Great Orton in 1829, fathered ten children.

The International Genealogical Index tells us very little of the births marriages and deaths, after about 1850, but from the Census of 1881, we do know that the eldest son of Joseph and Margaret, Jeremiah, born in 1832, married Mary Holmes, at Great Orton, in 1856, that she was a widow by 1881, and that she, a domestic servant, aged 40, was living at Lorne Street, Carlisle, with five children, Jane, 21 steamloom weaver, Joseph 18, a railway clerk, Ann 15, another steamloom weaver, Hannah, 10 and Thomas, 7,being scholars. Of course there could have been other children, who at the census time were living away from home. Also recorded in the 1881 census were Thomas, Joseph and Margaret's youngest, aged 25, general labourer, with his young wife Margaret, aged 23. They lived at Whinnow, Thursby. At Curthwaite there was a Maggie, aged 17, grand-daughter of Joseph and Margaret - their daughter, Martha had given birth to an illegitimate child in 1863.

Most of the family branches of Huntingtons lived within a few miles of Carlisle, and must therefore have very aware of, if not directly affected by, the events surrounding the two Jacobite risings. This particular branch, living in Great Orton, whose parish boundary marches with that of St. Mary's Carlisle, must have been extremely conscious of the goings-on.

The first rising, in 1715, occurred after Queen Anne, who had reigned since 1702, died in 1714. She was succeeded on the throne by the Hanoverian George. This had been provided for in the 1701 Act of Settlement, which named his mother, Sophia, the Electress of Hanover, (and her heirs and successors) as sovereign. Sophia was the youngest daughter of Elizabeth, the daughter of James I, Queen Anne having no children. Sophia had died, and George, the Elector of Hanover, who spoke no English was accepted as the rightful heir. The other claimant to the throne was James Edward, the Old Pretender, the son of James II, who had died in exile. In 1715 he landed in Scotland to claim the throne. His supporters, called the Jacobites, were mainly from Scotland, Ireland, and the North of England, where Roman Catholic adherants were still numerous. France, also supportive of the catholic claim, gave help both morally and in material terms by sending troops. A rising in Northumberland, under Sir John Forster fizzled out, and one in the west, though planned, came to nothing, after news of the defeat of James's supporters at Sheriffmuir. The local militia were mobilised, but although a few people lost their heads, the first Jacobite rising subsided.

The second Jacobite rising, in 1745, was more serious. In July Prince Charles Edward Stuart, grandson of James II, landed in Scotland, again with the support of the French, and gathered a lot of enthusiastic support about him. He defeated the English army at Preston Pans, near Edinburgh, travelled south with his army, and before long was besieging Carlisle, which surrendered within a few days. Although much scorn was afterwards heaped on the defenders, for their failure to resist, the garrison comprised less than a hundred old soldiers, invalids, 'very old and infirm', and about 500 militia, scraped up from Cumberland and Westmorland, plus 61 mounted soldiers. A later inspection of their nominal rolls revealed how poorly they were prepared for fighting, with comments such as : 'no sword', 'gun bad', 'wants a bayonet', 'quite incomplete'. These were supposed to defend the city walls whose perimeter was about 700 yards. Perhaps these militia men could not really be blamed; right down to today there are people who are willing to have others die that a faith or cause shall prevail. History records that the invading soldiers behaved well to the citizens of Carlisle during their short stay, before continuing their march southwards. The rebel army took Manchester, and advanced as far as Derby, on their way to London. There was great alarm in London, but in the event their fears were needless, for at Derby the Young Pretender turned back. It is probable that he had counted on more support than he received in England, and decided that he had better consolidate his success in Scotland. In other words he scaled down his objective.

But first he had to get back to Scotland in safety, and the mauling which his army received on his return journey through Westmorland and Cumberland must have magnified its demoralisation The retreat took place in December 1745, and the exposure of the troops to the unmerciful weather in this hill country, must have been bad enough, without the fierce skirmishes to which they were subjected at Clifton Moor, near Penrith, at Temple Sowerby, Culgaith, Langwathby, along the course of the river Eden, and again near Carlisle. For this period 1745/6, the parish registers of Carlisle, and surrounding parishes, record numerous burials of soldiers and rebels who had died in these fights. Although the Highlanders had not molested the country people of Westmorland and Cumberland on their progress southwards, they themselves were continually harrassed by the country folk on their way back to Scotland, and to their eventual defeat at Culloden. Many of these people regarded the affair as 'Sunday hunting'. No molestation perhaps but there is little doubt that the sufferers, were the villagers in the path of the retreating highlanders, who would have been plundered of their stocks of food. It was recorded that, on news of the approach of the highlanders towards Penrith, the citizens of that town took up arms to cut off stragglers, and that Dalston and Sebergham fielded strong parties, armed as best they could, to guard the Sebergham bridges. One group of highlanders, knowing that their path via Penrith was blocked, tried to escape to Scotland by the route along the eastern bank of the river Eden. Crossing the Eden at Temple Sowerby, they made for Culgaith and then Langwathby. But the Penrith men forestalled this by crossing the Eden lower down at Langwathby Bridge. A number of the country men came across the highlanders on Langwathby Moor, shots were fired,and the highlanders were hustled, once again southward. Back they went through Culgaith, and Newbiggin, until they reached Kendal. They then turned northwards again with more resolve and rejoined their main force near Penrith, where at Clifton, a fierce and bloody skirmish took place, before they could extricate themselves, and make their escape towards Carlisle.

Here ends, for the time being, our knowledge of further happenings to this branch of Huntingtons. It is very much hoped that this book might, in the future, stimulate members of the family to make themselves known, so that the story can be brought up to date.

HUNTINGTON PLACE, GREAT ORTON.
ONCE THE SITE OF MAINSFOLD?
PHOTOGRAPH BY KINDNESS OF MR. WILSON SWAN, OF CARLISLE.

CHAPTER FIVE

THE MAN WHO WAS THURSBY
(With apologies to G.K.Chesterton)

"THURSBY, like Thursday, is said to have derived its name from the pagan god Thor, dedicated to which deity here is said to have been a temple at the place now called Woodrigs, where the foundations were dug up about 55 years ago"

So commented the editor of William Hutchinson's History of Cumberland, published in 1797. He also named the late John Studholme, of Moorend, Thursby, as the famous son of Thursby, who had been living in the parish, up to his 85th year, in 1795, and who had published a 'Moral Essay' which the Westminster Magazine of 1779, described as being " a very ingenious and philosophic piece, written with both intelligence and intelligibility."

A note of interest is that Dorothy Huntington,of Thursby, married a John Studholme of Thursby in 1676, and that a John Studholme, son of John and Dorothy, was baptised at Thursby in November 1678.It seems that Dorothy died, perhaps in childbirth, because John Studholme married Mabel Huntington at Westward in 1679.

Thursby village is situated about 6 miles south-west of Carlisle, and about 4 ½ miles east of Wigton. It is bounded by the parishes of Dalston to the east,Westward to the south, Wigton to the west and by the parishes of Aikton and Great Orton to the north. Inevitably a number of the lives described in this chapter were not spent exclusively in the parish of Thursby, as the families spilled over the parish boundaries in all directions. Indeed many of the land holdings which had been cultivated by the Thursby Huntingtons were in Westward Parish, at the Curthwaites , Howrigg and Townhead.

Hutchinson's History describes Thursby in aspect as "situated rather low, and in general is level". It reports laconically "No dissenters". The small school had been endowed with £354 left in 1798 by Thomas Tomlinson, of North Carolina, once a native of Thursby. The population in 1797 was given as 446, with the information that, in the past 20 years, there had been 186 baptisms, and 98 burials. However it should be remembered that infant mortality was high in those times.

A further comment in the History of Cumberland tells us that: "The figure of the parish is rather of a triangular form. At a place called Nealehouse Bars, on the west side of Carlisle Moor, across the public road between Carlisle and Wigton, bars were anciently put up. Almost very village in northern parts of Cumberland have remains of these bars to this day. They were strong upright posts, and iron chains fixed into them, which went across the entrances into villages, to secure their cattle and other valuables in the night from the Moss-Troopers.(The raiders from across the Solway Firth). Besides these bars, each village had a watchman; and many a story is told of the conflicts between the villagers and marauders." The historian was in an informative mood, and continued: "The spirit of husbandry is very prevalent here; few parishes in the county have made a more rapid progress therein. - There are only two persons in the parish licensed to sell spiritous liquors and ale. The people here are in general sober and industrious, many of whom are independent." And he added:

"Common wages for labourers in husbandry, by day are 10d., Carpenters and Masons, from 1/2d to 1/6d., tailors 10d., when victuals are found them. The usual fuel is coals, which cost 3/6d per cart load." Then more tourist-promotion:" There is a singular piece of ground, on the eastern boundary, called Cardew Mire, but the original name was Carthieu, or God's Bog". It was remarkably boggy within the memory of man, but now the ground is drained, and become meadowland".

CHART NO.6
THE HUNTINGTONS FROM THURSBY

We start with Thomas Huntington, who was baptised at Thursby, on 17th May, 1663. We have speculated in chapter 3 on his prior ancestry, speculation being necessary because of the interruption of church record-keeping, during the mid-seventeenth century.

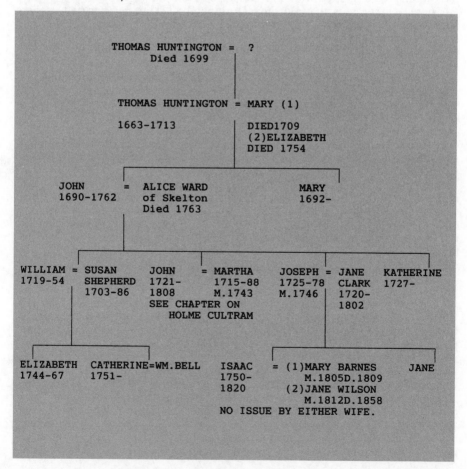

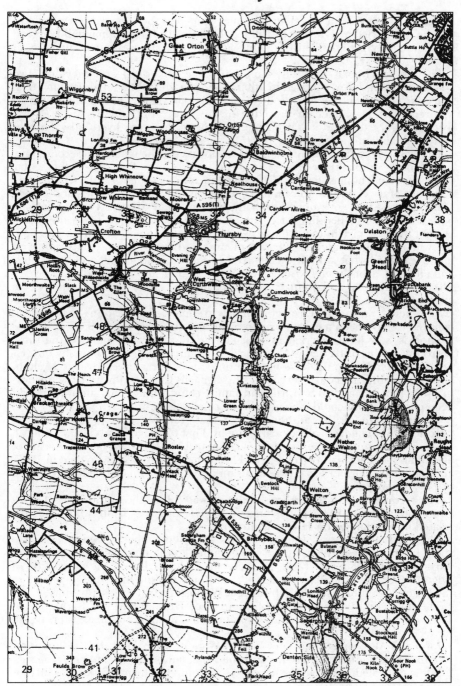

Little is known about the elder Thomas, named at the top of the tree, except that he was buried at Thursby in 1699. A Thomas Huntington married Margrett Bridge, in July 1661,at Penrith, Saint Nicholas, and she was buried in 1678, at Thursby.

Their son, Thomas married Mary (Surname unknown) and they had two children - a son, John, baptised in 1690, and a daughter, Mary, baptised in 1692. Mary survived childhood, but died, aged 23, in 1715. The family lived at Moorend, a tiny hamlet on the edge of the village of Thursby. Many of the dwellings still exist, and it is probable that one of them was lived in by Thomas and his small family.

Thomas' wife Mary died in 1709, and it appears that he married a second time, for although no marriage record has been found in the Parish Registers so far studied, when Thomas died in 1713, he bequeathed as follows: " I give unto my daughter Mary eight pound of money, to be payed by my executors, and I leave Mary one chest. "I give unto Elizabeth, my wife, and Mary, my daughter, one bed, and sufficient bedding of cloaths, and one iron pot, all these they have betwixt them. "I give unto my daughter Mary, one Counter. I give unto Elizabeth my wife, one chest, and all the rest of my goods and chattels, moveable and immoveable, of what kind or quality so ever they may be found, and bookdebts, and all other debts in any wise belonging to me, I clearly and absolutely give to Elizabeth, my wife, and John Huntington, my son, which two I joyne my sole executors..............."

The newly widowed Elizabeth shortly re-married, to John Huntington, believed to have been a cousin by marriage, and she lived on until 1754.

Thomas' son John married in February 1716, in fact he married the same person twice, his bride being Alice Ward. They first married at Thursby on 21st February, then they must have hopped onto an ox-cart, driven over to Skelton, and had another marriage service at St. Michael's Church. Presumably this was in order that Mr. and Mrs Ward, and family could witness that all honour had been observed, and could take part in the celebrations.

The marriage of the author's 6 x Great-grandparents, John and Alice, produced four children, all born at Thursby. First to arrive was William, in 1719. He married Susannah Shepherd, at Wigton, in 1743, she then being 37 years of age, to his 24. They had two children, Elizabeth, born in 1744, who died in 1767, and Catherine, born in 1751, (when Susannah was 45), who married William Bell in 1777, at Wigton.

The second of John and Alice's children was John, (the author's 5 x Great-Grandfather) born in 1721, destined to have a long and fruitful life, which is related in the chapter on Holme Cultram.

The third child born to John and Alice was Joseph, who arrived in 1725. He spent his adult life in Wigton, at a small hamlet to the north of the town, called Tarnrigg, abbreviated to Tarig, and later to Oulton, also on the north side of Wigton. Joseph was a Shoemaker, and from time to time his name appeared in the Church Register as a Churchwarden. We shall return to Joseph shortly.

The final child to be born to John and Alice Huntington, was Katherine, in 1727, but no further mention of her has been found so far in the registers which have been studied.

John and Alice spent their later lives in Wigton, where they died within a few months of each other, John dying in June 1762, and Alice, in January 1763.

When they died, their eldest surviving son, John, was living a few miles further to the west, in the parish of Holme Cultram, and their youngest son, Joseph, was living in Wigton, with his wife Jane (Clark), whom he had married in 1746, at Wigton. They had only two children, Isaac, born in 1750, and Jane.

Joseph died in 1778, aged 53, at Wigton, and left a will as follows: "....First,I leave, give and bequeath, to Jane, my beloved wife,the sum of one hundred and sixty pounds, current British money, (about £8000 in current values) with two feather beds, and the linning and wooling cloaths belonging to them. Also I leave, give and bequeath, to my son, Isaac, all the rest, residue, and remainder of my lands, goods, and chattels, moveable and immoveable, that is now or hereafter may become due to me, and do here constitute and make him my full and sole executor ....Joseph Huntington, his mark."

So whereas Joseph's grandfather Thomas had, 65 years previously, left his wife Elizabeth, and her stepdaughter Mary, to share one bed between them, Joseph was able to bequeath his wife Jane, the luxury of two beds, fully equipped, to say nothing of the princely sum of one hundred and sixty pounds current British money! And Isaac had "all his lands, etc.,..." Clearly Joseph had been quite a successful shoemaker. His wife Jane lived on for a further 14 years, dying at the age of 82, in 1802, at Oulton.

Isaac Huntington, Joseph and Jane's son, described himself as a Yeoman, presumably farming the land which his father bequeathed to him. Isaac's name appears from time time as Churchwarden, as had his father's. He did not marry until he was 55, and obviously was content to live at home with his widowed mother Jane, until she died in 1802. Then in 1805 he married Mary Barnes at Wigton. Sadly she died, aged 47, in 1809. One wonders whether she died in childbirth. Then in 1812, Isaac married Jane Wilson, but of course he was destined to die without issue, and he died in 1820, aged 70. He left a long will, appointing trustees, and leaving the sum of three hundred pounds for them to invest, the income to go to his wife Jane, for as long as she did not re-marry. In that event, he directed that the legacy should go to his next of kin, "whoever they may be and wherever they may be" He left outright to Jane all his property, lands, rights etc. and it is clear that Jane was able to live a widowhood at least clear of financial worries. Jane is one of my favourite characters in this story; she lived on until 1858 at Oulton. She too left a will, and being childless, it is heart-warming to read that she left a substantial sum to her niece by marriage, Margaret Hutton, (nee Huntington), the illegitimate daughter of her cousin by marriage, Mary Huntington, whose lives are described in the next chapter, and referred to in chapter 10. It is interesting to find such links, as the mere records in the parish registers only state bald isolated facts. A further point of interest is that one of the trustees appointed by Isaac Huntington was a Joseph Skelton, again almost certainly a connection with the Holme Cultram family.

Because Joseph and Jane Huntington's family line had come to a cul de sac with the childless marriages of Isaac, and John and Alice's elder son William's offspring had produced only girls, the continuation of the Huntington name, by this branch of the family was left to their second son,John, and his wife, Martha, who, as mentioned before, were living in Holme Cultram. As will be seen, they made up generously for any shortfall elsewhere in this respect.

ABOVE: THURSBY VILLAGE WITH OLD SCHOOL.

BELOW: ST. ANDREW'S THURSBY.

Another famous son of Thursby was Sir Thomas Bouch, (1822-1880). He was one of the five children of William Bouch, whose career had included yeoman farmer, licensee of the Ship Inn, and the captaincy in the merchant service, sailing from the West Cumberland ports. Thomas's elder brother William, became a distinguished locomotive engineer on the Stockton and Darlington Railway, and Thomas joined him there in 1845.

He had shown an aptitude for mechanics at his local school in Thursby, (yet one more sign of the superior quality of the Cumbrian schooling) where he was encouraged by the teacher, Mr. Joseph Hannah, an enthusiastic follower of current technological advances. He went then to the Abbey Street School in Carlisle, after which he took up a post with a mechanical engineering company in Liverpool. Later still he became apprenticed as a land surveyor to a firm of civil engineers,Larmer and Errington, working on the Lancaster and Carlisle Railway. Following this he became manager of the Edinburgh and Northern Railway, where he set about making the company efficient. As Resident Engineer he studied the problems of crossing the Forth and the Tay estuaries by ferry. The route from Edinburgh to Dundee carried heavy freight, and Bouch refined a previous design to create the first floating railway in the world. This set him off in his career, and he later established a private practice in Edinburgh, designing, in subsequent years over 250 miles of Railway in the north of England, and Scotland. He also designed several remarkable bridges, which included the Belah Viaduct (1040 ft. long), and the Deepdale Viaduct, near Kirkby Stephen, (740 ft. long, and 161 ft. high)

The crowning achievement of his career should have been the Tay Bridge, completed in 1879. At 2 miles long, it was the longest railway bridge in the world. Queen Victoria travelled over it in that year, on her way south from Balmoral. He was knighted, and he immediately formed a company to build a bridge over the Forth.

Disaster struck in December of the same year, when, whilst a train was passing over the bridge, a terrific gale caused it to collapse. The crew and 75 passengers died in this tragedy. An enquiry by the Board of Trade revealed alarming shortcomings, not in the design, but in the materials used, and in the supervision of the bridge construction. Unfairly, many thought, Sir Thomas Bouch was made the scapegoat, and bore the brunt of the blame. In 1880 Sir Thomas Bouch died at Moffat, a brilliant career blighted by the disaster.

SIR THOMAS BOUCH

THURSBY 1920: THE THREE STOREY BUILDING ON THE RIGHT
IS THE HOUSE WHERE SIR THOMAS BOUCH LIVED

THATCHED HOUSE IN CURTHWAITE, BUILT 1666,
RE-THATCHED IN 1992 PREVIOUSLY WAS A FARMHOUSE.

Thursby

CHAPTER SIX

THE PARISH OF HOLME CULTRAM
(In Allerdale Ward below Derwent)

" Here was an abbey of Cistercians, but there is now very little of the monastic buildings; and but a part of the church, in its original form, is standing: the parochial chapel was formed out of its remains. It is said by several writers, that this abbey was founded by Prince Henry, son of David, King of Scotland, about the year 1150"

Thus quoted William Hutchinson's History of Cumberland, in 1797. He also quoted other sources which suggested that the founder was King Henry I, which if true would date the foundation back to before 1135. During the period of the dissolution of the monastery, and the later period of the Reformation, the Church suffered much damage and neglect, culminating, at the beginning of the 17th century, with a singular event described in the Parish Register as follows: "The steeple of the Church, being of the height of nineteen fathoms, suddenly fell down to the ground, upon the fifth day of January, in the year 1600, about three o'clock in the afternoon, and by the fall thereof, brought down a great part of the chancel, both timber, lead and walls, and, after the said fall, the same continued in a very ruinous condition for the space of two years, during which time there was much lead, wood, and stone carried away." Work started on the rebuilding in 1602 and 1603, but more mishap occurred in 1604, when "It so happened that Wednesday, 18th April, 1604, one Christopher Hardon carrying a live coal and a candle into the roof of the church, to search for an iron chisel which his brother had left there, and the wind being exceeding strong and boistrous, it chanced that the coal flew out of his hand into a Daw's nest, which was within the roof of the church, which kindled the flame, which set the roof on fire, and within less than three hours it consumed and burned both the body of the chancel, and the whole church, except the south side of the low church, which was saved by means of a stone vault"

A charge was brought against Mr Mandevil, the builder, and his servant Christopher Hardon, for burning the church wilfully and maliciously, but failing proof, the charge was dismissed. Mr Mandevil, at his own cost, voluntarily rebuilt the chancel, and the parishoners repaired the church.

The historian could not resist adding his own observation that "carrying live coals to give light to search for the carpenter's tools, looks more like mischievous intention than folly." He adds the further damning comment: "A correspondent informs us that Harding was employed to shoot jackdaws - even during the time of divine service".

Over the years, the Parish Register frequently notes the condition of the church, and it is also possible to realise from other entries, that the people of this parish were kept well aware of events occurring far from their remote homeland. Thus, in 1692, "collected 1/5d for those suffering by fire in Ledbury" "Collected 3/2d for the suffering by casualties at sea" In December 1692, "collected 1/5 1/2d for the suffering by fire in Chagford" And in 1694 "collected in October for ye relief of French Protestants, who were exiled out of their native country, the sum of £8.7.10d" and in the same month, "collected the sum of 9/1d for the captives in Algeria, in the dominion of Fez in Morrocco" and "collected for the inhabitants of Thirsk, in the north riding of York, who suffered by fire, 2/1d"

And they could look inwards too; each year the churchwardens were required to make 'presentments' by which they notified the Bishop of any delinquents within their parish, a duty their relishing of which seemed sometimes very obvious: 1672. "We the churchwardens do present John Barns and Thomas Wilkinson for not bringing their children to be baptised, according to Church Government." "We present John Parkin and Jane Howell for keeping house together, and living unmarried" "We present the following for denying to pay their several portions of the tax for repairing the church: Thomas Stordie, William Saull, John Taylor, and Richard Miller" "We present Thomas Wilkinson (clearly a bad lot!)of the Abbey, and William Robinson for working in their shoppe on Christmas Day in time of divine service and sermon" (The pioneers of Sunday Trading). "Also we present Sir William Dalston, Knight, and Baronet, for not repairing the chancel at Abbey Holme"

The parish of Holme Cultram is large in area, extending a distance of about 13 miles from the mouth of the River Wampoul, to Allonby, a one time seaside resort. So on the west it is bounded by the ocean, on the north by the estuary, and Solway Firth, on the south by the parish of Bromfield, and on the east by the parishes of Wigton and Kirkbride. Low Holme is a level marshy and sandy tract, and most of the parish is fairly plain and level, well ditched to provide drainage. It has numerous hamlets, mainly small, such as Angerton,Bitterlees, Calvo,Long Newton, Low Holme, Moss-side, Pelutho,Raby, Silloth, and Skinburness, Southerfield, and Wolsty.

The 1829 Directory listed a large number of citizens with a variety of trades, as well as farmers and yeomen. Amongst these names are many familiar to anyone who has studied the parish registers of two hundred years earlier: Messenger, Drape, Glaister, Pape, Biglands, Hayton, Jefferson, Langcake, Peat, Saul Tordiff, Twentyman, Younghusband, Ritson, Huddart, and, amongst the farmers, JONATHAN SKELTON. Here is a list of the citizens of Abbey Holme in 1829, giving their occupations:

Bewley,Thomas, Tailor,
Collinson,Rev.Robert,
perpetual curate,Parsonage Ho.
Garner, Thomas, Cooper.
Hewetson, William Ross,Schoolmr.
Pape, Daniel, Joiner
Scott, Robert, Nailmaker
Pape, Jesse, Letters Inn
Harrison, William,Wheatsheaf Inn.
Olivant, William, Shoemaker.

Brough,John, Blacksmith
Dawson, Daniel, Stonemason
Drape, John, Surgeon.
Glaister, William, Gentleman
Messenger, Mrs. Mary, Kingside.
Richardson, George,corn miller
Brough,Joseph, Duke's Head
Osborne, William, Oak Tavern
Brough, Hudson, Grocer
Pape, Joseph,Shoemaker.

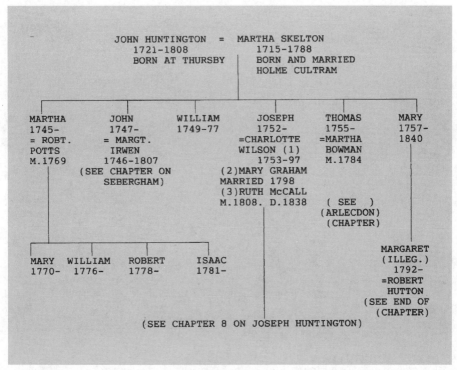

THE HUNTINGTONS FROM THE PARISH OF HOLME CULTRAM
CHART NO.7

John Huntington came from the Thursby branch of Huntingtons, believed to be one of the, if not the, original places of settlement by the surname. John was the second son of three born to John and Alice Huntington of Thursby. He chose to be a Weaver, and when he grew up he moved to an area west of Wigton, in the parish of Holme Cultram, where, at the age of 21 he married Martha Skelton, then aged 28. The Skeltons, particularly in that corner of Cumbria, formed quite a large family group, judging by the events recorded in the Parish Register. They married in March 1743.

John and Martha, as can be noted from the family tree above, and some trees detailed in other chapters, were destined to found several branches of Huntingtons, which penetrated into, and settled in, parts of Cumbria new to them.

At the time of their marriage, John and Martha lived in the small township of Abbeytown , near the site of the ancient, ruined Abbey. Abbeytown is and was the most substantial settlement in a large area, bordered on its North and West by the Solway estuary, and comprising numerous small hamlets, and much scrubby waste land. It stands near the River Waver, which rises to the south of Westward and Wigton, and meanders across the flatlands, to its marshy estuary on the Solway, north of Abbeytown.

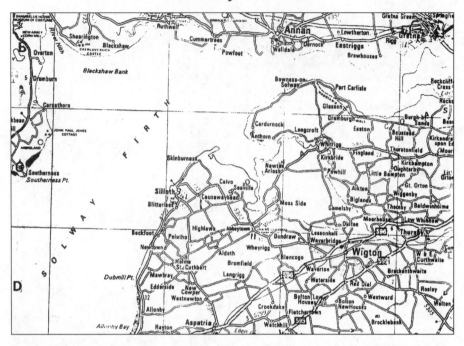

BELOW: ABBEYTOWN
HOLME CULTRAM ABBEY
FOUNDED IN 1150.

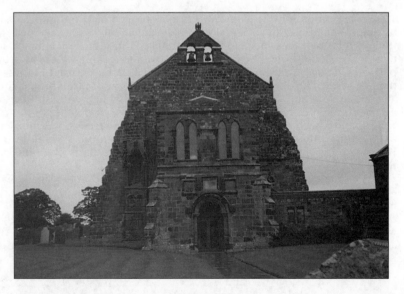

Their first child, Martha, was born in May 1745, followed by John, the writer's Great-great-great-great-grandfather, in June, 1747, and by William, in 1749. Up to this date the address of John and Martha had always been recorded as 'of Abbeytown'. When Joseph was baptised in July 1752, however, their address was given as 'Swinstis'. A Swinsty Farm exists about half a mile south of Abbeytown, and it is possible of course, that they had been living there all the while, but that the clerk recording the latest birth had a taste to be more informative than his predecessor. Next, in March 1755, came Thomas, and the address given now was Southerfield, which is shewn on current maps as comprising two or three dwellings at most, there being close by Southerfield Hall, and Southerfield House, as well as a 'Weary Hall'. Indeed Martha must have getting a little weary when her last child, Mary, was born in October 1757.

The next event to be recorded at Holme Cultram was the marriage of young Martha, at the age of 24, to Robert Potts, described as a manservant, in November 1769. Could he have been a manservant at nearby Southerfield Hall or Southerfield House? They produced four children : Mary in September 1770, William in 1776, Robert in 1778, when the address of Robert and Martha was given as 'Pelatho' The hamlet of Pelutho lies about 3 miles south and east of Abbeytown, and again nearby there are Pelutho Grange and Pelutho Park, and possibly Robert and Martha were in service at one of these. The last Potts to arrive was Isaac, baptised in September 1781, when the parents still lived at 'Pelathoe'

In 1770 the eldest son of John and Martha, John was married to Margaret (Peggy) Irwen at Westward, seven miles away, and they were to make their home, and to bring up their family in the village of Sebergham. Their lives, and those of their descendants are covered by chapter 9.

In 1777 the second son of John and Martha, William, died at the age of 27, and the address of the family was still given as Southerfield. Number three son, Joseph, was married at Holme Cultram in November 1778, when he was aged 26. His bride was Charlotte Wilson. Joseph was to father in all twelve children, of which eight were by Charlotte. Joseph's family is covered by chapter 8, and the lives of John and Martha's youngest son Thomas, who married Martha Bowman in 1784 in Arlecdon, are related in chapter 7.

John Huntington became a widower when his wife Martha died in June 1788, aged 73, at a place with the salubrious name of Bog. This is shewn on the map as a dwelling, or small farm about two miles down the road from Southerfield. Maybe she was being nursed at Bog during an illness, but we know that John still stayed at Southerfield, and that he was looked after by his youngest daughter, Mary, for this was the address for them given in January 1792, when Mary's illegitimate daughter, Margaret, was baptised, the father being named as Joseph Wilkinson.

BELOW:PELUTHO HOME OF ROBERT AND MARTHA (NEE HUNTINGTON) POTTS

BELOW: BOG FARM

Mary, at this time, was no ignorant, easily seducible young thing. She was 34 years old, and for nearly four years, at the least, she had been running the home, following her mother's death, and looking after her father, by then aged 70. Looking back from the twentieth century, we still look at things with the inherited mores of the Victorian age, which stand between our time and that of the eighteenth century. We forget that the Victorian scale of values was in large part a reaction from the scandalous attitudes and behaviour, under a veil of respectability, of the nobility, and the monied class, which had reached rock-bottom in Britain in the days of the Prince-to-be- Prince-Regent-to-be-King George IV, and which itself had mirrored the behaviour of the Bourbons on the continent of Europe. The matter of illegitimacy was regarded with a great deal of indulgence in the eighteenth century, particularly if the end result was a wedding. Perhaps time will permit more comment on this subject later.

This particular illegitimacy did not result in a wedding for Mary; probably Joseph Wilkinson was already married. Mary's daughter Margaret was brought up in what today is called a 'single parent family', that is, disregarding Margaret's grandfather, who by then was 71. The love that Margaret attracted is instanced by the fact that when old John Huntington eventually died, in 1808, aged 86, he left the major part of his estate to Mary, and for her daughter Margaret. In addition,in the 1858 will of Jane Huntington, the widow of her childless marriage to Isaac Huntington, and second cousin by marriage to Margaret bequeathed the not inconsiderable sum , for those days, of fifty pounds.

Returning to the will of John Huntington, if length of the contents of a will are any criterion, then Old John must have died quite a wealthy man. Unfortunately we do not have an inventory to the will, and can only surmise that he must have had a successful weaving career, such that he must have employed other people. By the time of making his will John, Mary, and Margaret were living in Wigton, at Dockwrayrigg House, Oulton. In the first instance he bequeaths "To my daughter Mary, who now lives with me,one half of that property at Cardewlees, in the parish of Dalston, and of all my possessions elsewhere in Cumberland" To his grand-daughter, Margaret Huntington, he left the sum of £40,(about £2000 in 1995 money) to be paid to her when she reached the age of 21,or when she married, if earlier. The money meantime was to be invested to pay for her education. Of the residue he directed that this be divided into five equal parts, and that his five surviving 'children', including Mary, should each have one fifth. Mary also inherited all of his household goods and personal belongings. John was rightly very grateful to his youngest daughter, and clearly wanted his Grand-daughter Margaret to be free from want. The reference to 'the property at Cardewlees is intriguing, and possibly one day some more light on this may be obtainable from the successors in business of Silas Saul, Attorneys at Law. It is believed that there were some weaving establishments at Cardewlees. The matter becomes more intriguing as John Huntington bequeathed £50 "To Matthewson Hodgson, and a further £5 in token of thanks to him for his many kindnesses, and any money due to Silas Saul 'for defending my rights of title to the property at Cardewlees'".

John Huntington had been fortunate in his career as weaver, because the latter part, at least, had spanned a period of great prosperity for the textile industry, particularly boosted, no doubt by the continental wars with Napoleon, and by the huge increase in the production of yarn from the spinning mills. At this period weaving was done by handloom, which could involve whole families, wives as well as children in the industry. Weavers, at that time , constituted the third largest occupational group in the country. In Wigton alone there were reported to be 120 handloom weavers, and this figure was probably underestimated. In the outlying hamlets and villages, Oulton included, where Dockwrayrigg House is situated, there were many more weavers, mainly employed as outworkers, working at looms in their own homes. (The present owner of Dockwrayrigg House told the author that when he bought the property several years ago, there had been clear evidence that part of them had been used for weaving.)

These weavers would supply the finished cloth to manufacturers in Wigton, such as Isaac Pattinson, Thomas Bushby, Daniel Hewson, J.Reed, or Hodges, and at the same time would collect their yarn to weave their next bolt of cloth.

BELOW: ONE OF THE LAST HANDLOOM WEAVING MACHINES IN WIGTON. THIS HAD BELONGED TO WILLIAM DODGSON, WHO EMPLOYED A NUMBER OF WEAVERS AT HIS PREMISES IN WATER STREET. PHOTOGRAPH TAKEN IN THE 1890S.
BY KIND PERMISSION OF MR. TREVOR GRAHAMSLAW OF WIGTON.

Within a couple of decades after John's death in 1808, however, the situation began to change drastically; the power loom was introduced, and this together with the economic circumstances in the 1820s, put vast numbers of operatives in the textile trade out of work. Dreadful conditions of poverty among formerly prosperous tradesmen prevailed. Eventually these conditions led to rioting, and calls for a People's Charter. Countrywide, the Chartist movement led to alarm, rioting, and often culminated in military intervention to quell disturbances. Although places like Wigton and Carlisle were touched by these troubles, they were mild compared with many other parts of the country, such as in the southern counties, where some rioters were hanged, hundreds, including young people in their teens were transported to the colonies as punishment, and hundreds others were imprisoned. Thus we can observe the steady decline in one of the major occupational activities of Cumberland, indeed of the country, over quite a short span of time, matched by the depredations in work availability for those dependent on agriculture for a living, as first, land enclosures drove many independent farmers and statesmen to become labourers, and then the agricultural revolution, with its emphasis on farm mechanisation, reduced the demand for farm labourers. These factors, coinciding with the essentially urban-based Industrial Revolution, caused country people increasingly to flock to the towns and cities, in order to make a living, where they in turn caused the labour supply to exceed demand, and eventually suffered another cycle of hardship, and to give rise to a new type of squalor - that of overcrowded slums.

The weavers and textile workers had been among the first groups to attempt to organise themselves in trade associations, and were therefore among the first also to encounter governmental opposition to efforts at such self-protection. In 1799, legislation was enacted to suppress such combinations of workers, even though the action they took, usually consisting of organising 'memorials', or petitions to their employers, was moderate by later standards. Only when these endeavours failed would they usually resort to strikes or food riots. As it became clear that Parliament was supportive of their employers, the weavers realised that only a radical political stance might be able to halt the deterioration of their condition. This is the road which they eventually took, despite the difficulties which groups of outworkers encountered in welding themselves into a trade association.

We should note that we, two hundred years later, have not mastered the problems of hardship and misery, caused by our ongoing Industrial Revolution. Our brilliantly inventive minds continuously evolve new technologies for reducing the labour content of our products and services, thus effectively creating unemployment, and perhaps we should devote much more of this human ability to making compensatory provision of useful work for those sections of the populace whom our innovations make redundant.

ABOVE: DOCKWRAYRIGG HOUSE,OULTON, NEAR WIGTON, WITH
WEAVING ROOMS AND STOREHOUSES AT SIDES.

This is an appropriate point at which to relate the story of Mary Huntington's descendants, which came to light in the course of an exchange of correspondence between parties who, unknown to one another who were researching this particular history. The writer lodged, with the Cumberland Family History Society, his interest in research of the Huntington family in Cumbria. A letter arrived from a lady in New Zealand, Mrs Lyn Harpham, that she had traced her family, on her Mother's side back to a Mary Huntington, baptised at Wigton in January 1818, the illegitimate daughter of Margaret Huntington, born at Holme Cultram. Margaret had later married Robert Hutton, a widower, a calico printer, in November 1824. This fitted in with the facts known; that Mary's daughter, Margaret, had in turn borne an illegitimate daughter Mary, (fathered by John Jennings, Weaver).

When Lyn Harpham knew all the facts that, between us, we were able to piece together, she was delighted on behalf of her ancestor, to know that Mary, her daughter Margaret, and in turn her daughter Mary, had been much loved members of their family. Some further reference to that branch of the Huntington family is made in the chapter on Skelton where paths crossed again, perhaps unbeknown to the parties.

Returning to the mainstream of the story, John Huntington's daughter lived on to the age of 83, dying in 1840, at Wigton. Her daughter, Margaret, as has been related, married Robert Hutton in 1824. This marriage produced three children, Martha, born in 1825, Hannah Maria, born in 1826, who married William Hutchinson, and Isabella, born in 1831, who married Joseph Johnson.

Mary married, in 1849, Anthony Wharton, a Saddler, and the marriage was at Wigton. Anthony and Mary had six children, and the first two, Margaret Ranger Wharton, and Elizabeth Wharton were baptised in 1849 and 1851 respectively, at Skelton, where other Huntington cousins had settled. Hannah Maria (Wharton), baptised in 1853, (the Grandmother of my correspondent, and sixth cousin, Mrs Lyn Harpham of New Zealand) was born to Anthony and Mary (nee Huntington) Wharton, and there followed Robert William in 1855, Jane Ann in 1857, and finally Isabella Ireland Wharton in 1860.

Margaret Ranger Wharton married Elijah Richardson at Temple Sowerby, Elizabeth married John Swainson; Lyn's Grandmother, Hannah Maria, married William Parkinson, at Durham, and he died at Croydon, Surrey, in 1937.

LEFT: THE PARKINSON FAMILY CIRCA 1910 AT NEWCASTLE-UPON-TYNE
BACK ROW: ETHEL, WILLIAM JNR, MABEL GEORGE AND MARY (LYN HARPHAM'S MUM)
FRONT ROW: HILDA, WILLIAM SNR, EDWARD, HANNAH-MARIA (LYN'S GRANDMOTHER) AND REBECCA. IT IS BELIVED THAT HENRY TOOK THE PHOTOGRAPH.
NOTE HANNAH MARIA WAS A DAUGHTER OF MARY WHARTON (NEE HUNTINGTON)

THE DESCENDANTS OF MARY HUNTINGTON (1757-1840)
OF HOLME CULTRAM.
CHART NO.8.

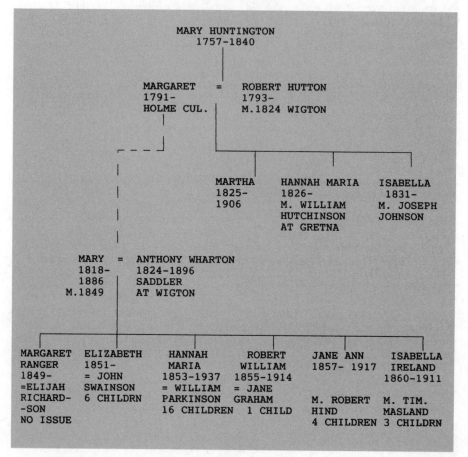

MARY HUNTINGTON
1757-1840

MARGARET   =   ROBERT HUTTON
1791-   1793-
HOLME CUL.   M.1824 WIGTON

MARTHA   HANNAH MARIA   ISABELLA
1825-   1826-   1831-
1906   M. WILLIAM   M. JOSEPH
            HUTCHINSON   JOHNSON
            AT GRETNA

MARY   =   ANTHONY WHARTON
1818-   1824-1896
1886   SADDLER
M.1849   AT WIGTON

| MARGARET RANGER 1849- =ELIJAH RICHARD--SON NO ISSUE | ELIZABETH 1851- = JOHN SWAINSON 6 CHILDRN | HANNAH MARIA 1853-1937 = WILLIAM PARKINSON 16 CHILDREN | ROBERT WILLIAM 1855-1914 = JANE GRAHAM 1 CHILD | JANE ANN 1857- 1917 M. ROBERT HIND 4 CHILDREN | ISABELLA IRELAND 1860-1911 M. TIM. MASLAND 3 CHILDRN |

CHAPTER SEVEN

THE HUNTINGTONS FROM THE PARISH OF ARLECDON
CHART NO.9

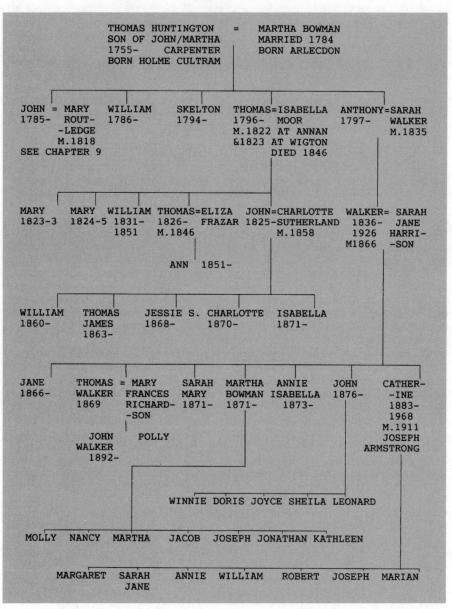

```
            THOMAS HUNTINGTON    =   MARTHA BOWMAN
            SON OF JOHN/MARTHA       MARRIED 1784
            1755-      CARPENTER     BORN ARLECDON
            BORN HOLME CULTRAM


JOHN = MARY    WILLIAM    SKELTON    THOMAS=ISABELLA   ANTHONY=SARAH
1785-  ROUT-   1786-      1794-      1796-  MOOR       1797-   WALKER
       -LEDGE                        M.1822 AT ANNAN           M.1835
       M.1818                        &1823 AT WIGTON
SEE CHAPTER 9                               DIED 1846


MARY     MARY    WILLIAM  THOMAS=ELIZA   JOHN=CHARLOTTE    WALKER= SARAH
1823-3   1824-5  1831-    1826-  FRAZAR  1825-SUTHERLAND   1836-   JANE
                 1851     M.1846              M.1858       1926    HARRI-
                                                           M1866   -SON

                          ANN   1851-


WILLIAM     THOMAS      JESSIE S.  CHARLOTTE   ISABELLA
1860-       JAMES       1868-      1870-       1871-
            1863-


JANE      THOMAS = MARY      SARAH    MARTHA    ANNIE     JOHN     CATHER-
1866-     WALKER   FRANCES   MARY     BOWMAN    ISABELLA  1876-    -INE
          1869     RICHARD-  1871-    1871-     1873-              1883-
                   -SON                                           1968
                                                                  M.1911
            JOHN        POLLY                                     JOSEPH
            WALKER                                               ARMSTRONG
            1892-


              WINNIE DORIS JOYCE SHEILA LEONARD


MOLLY  NANCY  MARTHA    JACOB   JOSEPH JONATHAN KATHLEEN


    MARGARET   SARAH      ANNIE   WILLIAM    ROBERT   JOSEPH   MARIAN
               JANE
```

THOMAS HUNTINGTON, the youngest son of John and Martha Huntington of Holme Cultram, was born in 1755. He became a carpenter, and married an Arlecdon girl, Martha Bowman, in 1784, at Arlecdon.Initially they lived at Waterend, a small hamlet at the northern end of Lake Loweswater,a couple of miles along the lake from the village of Loweswater, where some distant cousins, (Isaac and Sarah were living). Here, at Waterend their first son, John was born. But it was not long before they were living back in the parish of Arlecdon where Martha had been brought up, and where the next three of their children , William, Skelton, and Thomas were born. They were a mobile family, and had moved to Dalston. near the outskirts of Carlisle, by the time their last child was born in 1797.

The lives of his eldest son, John, and of his wife Mary (Routledge) are covered in chapter 9 on Sebergham, and little is so far known about the lives of their sons William and Skelton. Possibly they died in youth, or maybe they moved out of Cumberland, and beyond the scope of this research, to build their careers and lives.

Thomas, the fourth son of Thomas and Martha, had a romantic escapade; he eloped with Isabella Moor, in 1822, to be married in Annan, over the Scottish border. He was 26 years old, and Isabella was 32, so they did not do this because they were under- age. Perhaps the answer lies in the fact that their daughter, Mary, was born in the following April, seven months after their runaway marriage. Annan became popular, especially for nearby Cumbrians, for irregular marriages, at about that time, in preference to Gretna Green. It was much more attractive, compared with the rather squalid Gretna. The marriage procedure followed an ancient Scots statute, which made parties to an irregular marriage liable to a fine. This law was turned to a profitable use, with the co-operation of the magistrate. The couple would appear before him, and confess that they were irregularly married, that is, they had accepted one another as husband and wife, without banns or church ceremony. The magistrate would fine them a small amount of money, and issue a document with the equivalent of a marriage certificate. For a higher fee, and a contribution to the poor of the parish, he would hold a 'Kirk session' give them a telling off, confirm the marriage, and record the fact in the parish register. This procedure was stopped in 1824, and irregular marriages in Annan ceased.

It seems unlikely that Thomas and Isabella had the 'de Luxe' version, because they married 'again' in the following year at Wigton Parish Church. There was a doubly unhappy sequel, when their infant Mary died in that same year,1823, as did their next child, also baptised Mary in 1824, dying in 1825.

Thomas was a 'Waller' by trade, and this probably would have taken him about the region quite a lot. To the layman, the art of building dry stone walls may appear to be an easy one. A closer study of the construction of these walls, as they march up, down, and across the countryside, will destroy that illusion. Like his father, the carpenter, he moved about Cumberland to where the jobs demanding his skills were available, and presumably the progression of land enclosure made work plentifully available. Thomas and Isabella's third child, John, was born in 1825, and baptised in 1826, at Wigton. He married,in 1858, at the age of 33 Charlotte Sutherland, a young lady from Caithness, Scotland. John became a teacher, and the 1881 census records his address as The School House Court in Carlisle. With John and Charlotte the census records their children as being William, unmarried, aged 21, occupation Grocer, Thomas James, aged 18, occupation Pupil Teacher, Jessie S. (? Sutherland ?) 13 a scholar, Charlottenia, (hopefully the census enumerator's spelling mistake for Charlotte), aged 11, and Isabella, aged 10.

John Huntington, the schoolmaster died in 1887, and letters of administration were taken out by his widow. John's grandparents, Thomas, the carpenter, and Martha, as well as his parents, Thomas the wall builder, and Isabella, must have been proud that John had made it as a teacher in Cumberland's capital city.

John's calling as a teacher must have been a difficult one; an Education Committee was set up in Carlisle in 1854, and the secretary of the committee drew a grimly revealing picture of the inadequate schools, widely scattered, and lacking any sets of texts, beyond the Bible itself, with ' a few hacked and badly placed desks, tattered lesson cards, and broken slates'. They had to wait for the 1870 Education Act before more adequate provision was to be made.

Thomas and Isabella's fourth child was Thomas, born in 1828, at Wigton. He was described as a labourer in a print works, in the 1851 Carlisle census. He married a Scots girl, Eliza Frazar, in 1846, and the 1851 census recorded that they then had a daughter, Ann, aged 2 months at the time of the census in April 1851. Living at the same address, at Parham Beck, was a 15 years old John Fraiser, described as a visitor, occupation Hand Loom Weaver, born in Scotland. Despite the difference in the spelling of his and Eliza's maiden name, he was very probably Eliza's young brother, seeking to make his life in England. Who knows? Maybe he was the ancestor of a fast bowler now playing cricket for England!!

The last of Thomas and Isabella's children was William, born in 1831, at Wigton. Although he survived the dangers of infancy, he died as a young man of 20 in 1851.

In 1797 Thomas and Martha, with whom this story began, produced their fifth and last child, Anthony. He described himself as an Agricultural Labourer, and in 1835 he married Sarah Walker at Bridekirk. In an another chapter, reference is made to the fact that many marriages were being entered into much later in life, particularly where a man found it hard to make ends meet. Almost certainly this was the reason why Anthony did not marry until he was 38 years old. Probably this was also the reason that they only produced one child, baptised Walker in 1836. (There was an increasing trend to give one of the children their mother's maiden name). The 1881 census in Lamplugh, near Loweswater, records Anthony, aged 85, living with his son, Walker, aged 45, Agricultural Labourer, Walker's wife, Sarah Jane (nee Harrison), aged 36, whom he had married in 1866, and four of their six children, Thomas Walker, 12, Sarah Mary, 10, Martha Bowman,also aged 10, and John, aged 5. Absent from the tally were Jane, born in 1866, and Annie Isabella, born in 1873. It is possible that Jane who would be 15 if alive, was living away from home as a servant. Possibly both she and Annie had died in infancy.

Subsequently Thomas Walker, born in 1869, appears on the record as having married Mary Frances Richardson, at Frizington, and having baptised their son, John Walker, in 1892. It is likely that they had further children subsequently, as probably did Thomas and Eliza, after the birth of their Ann, in 1851. So this story which began in Arlecdon, saw the family disperse into many parts of Cumberland; Sebergham,Wigton, Carlisle, Dalston, and from those places, they doubtless spread far afield.

By way of a postscript to this chapter, a letter has been received from Mrs Margaret North, of Halton, near Lancaster, advising that she is a grand-daughter of Walker and Sarah Jane Huntington, (Walker, it transpires, lived until he was 90 years old, all but 6 days, dying on the 8th February 1926.)

Margaret North's mother, Catherine, was born in November 1883, and therefore did not appear on the 1881 census. Hopefully this will bring forth some more information on this branch of the family.

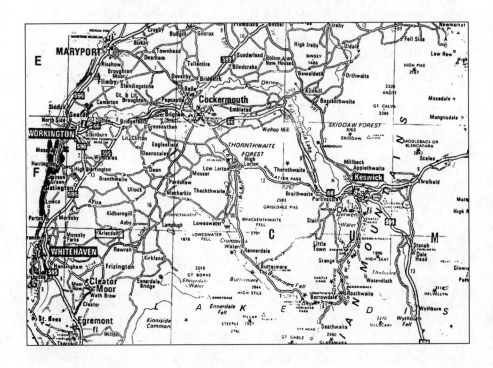

CHAPTER EIGHT

THE FAMILY OF JOSEPH HUNTINGTON
FROM HOLME CULTRAM AND OF BROMFIELD
BEWCASTLE CARLISLE AND WIGTON

CHART NO.10
JOSEPH HUNTINGTON

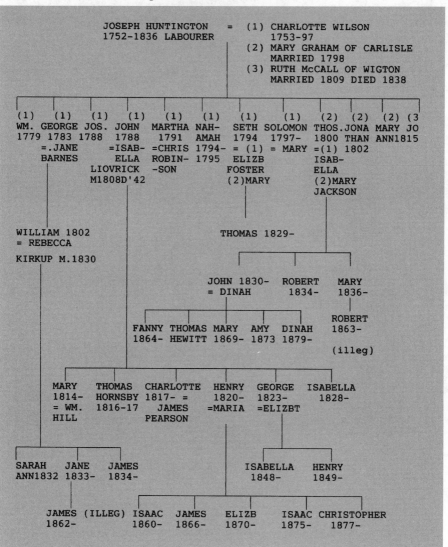

```
JOSEPH HUNTINGTON    =  (1) CHARLOTTE WILSON
1752-1836 LABOURER          1753-97
                        (2) MARY GRAHAM OF CARLISLE
                            MARRIED 1798
                        (3) RUTH McCALL OF WIGTON
                            MARRIED 1809 DIED 1838


(1)     (1)    (1)  (1)     (1)      (1)      (1)     (1)       (2)   (2)   (2) (3
WM.   GEORGE  JOS. JOHN   MARTHA  NAH-     SETH   SOLOMON  THOS.JONA MARY JO
1779   1783   1788 1788    1791   AMAH     1794   1797-    1800 THAN ANN1815
=.JANE              =ISAB-        1794-    = (1)  = MARY   =(1) 1802
BARNES              ELLA  =CHRIS  1795     ELIZB            ISAB-
                    LIOVRICK ROBIN-        FOSTER           ELLA
                    M1808D'42 -SON         (2)MARY          (2)MARY
                                                            JACKSON


WILLIAM 1802                    THOMAS 1829-
= REBECCA

KIRKUP M.1830
                         JOHN 1830-   ROBERT   MARY
                         = DINAH      1834-    1836-

                                                        ROBERT
                  FANNY THOMAS MARY  AMY  DINAH         1863-
                  1864- HEWITT 1869- 1873 1879-
                                                        (illeg)


     MARY    THOMAS   CHARLOTTE  HENRY   GEORGE  ISABELLA
     1814-   HORNSBY  1817- =    1820-   1823-   1828-
     = WM.   1816-17  JAMES      =MARIA  =ELIZBT
     HILL             PEARSON


SARAH   JANE   JAMES                  ISABELLA  HENRY
ANN1832 1833-  1834-                   1848-    1849-


      JAMES (ILLEG) ISAAC  JAMES  ELIZB    ISAAC CHRISTOPHER
      1862-         1860-  1866-  1870-    1875-  1877-
```

ST MARY'S PARISH CHURCH

"... And a very fair church in the markett towne of Wigton a little below; and heer you have a church on the more; no houses very nye though I think it be much frequented by people thereabout."
SANDFORD: HISTORY OF CUMBERLAND C.1675

This is one of the earliest references to the original church of St Mary, which was built by Wigton's first Lord of the Manor, Odard de Logis, early in the 12th century. Odard had the church built of stones carried from the Roman fort at Old Carlisle, some of which were carved and inscribed. There was extensive damage to the town and the church in the Scots raids of the early 14th century and by 1375/6 the tower of the church had been crenellated for defence – so the church may have looked very similar to the fortifed churches at Newton Arlosh and Burgh-by-Sands.

Carved head, probably from the old church, built into wash-house, Proctor's Row.

WIGTON OLD CHURCH: *"We know not the height, the length, nor the breadth of our Old Church, nor whether it possessed much of the hidden beauty we see in neighbouring churches; not even a sketch is left of its exterior."* said Wilson Moore in his *History and Topography of Wigton* in 1894. However, Willie Carrick, in his *History of Wigton*, makes an attempt to sketch his idea of the old church; note the very low nave and the fortified tower.

Left: ENGRAVING OF ST MARY'S CHURCH 1881: this was the year the interior of the church was extensively restored and decorated. The frame of the picture is supposedly made from oak recovered from the old church.

Below: CHURCH AND CORNMARKET, 1870s: with assorted worthies, who have obviously been asked to *pose* for the photograph. The lamp is the one which stood at the Market Place with the pump and is now in Wigton Park.

WINDOW FROM THE OLD CHURCH: a few relics of Odard's Church, this window among them, were erected in St Mary's church-yard after being rescued from various places around the town (the window had been built into the wall of a cottage at Mount Pleasant).

38

Reproduced by Kind Permission of Sue Allan

Joseph

The population of England doubled between 1750 and 1810, from about 5 million to about 10 million,and the need to feed these extra people helped to accelerate the Agricultural Revolution then under way.

Joseph Huntington and his succession of three wives, certainly played his part in that population explosion, fathering twelve children between 1779 and 1815. They in their turn blessed him with about eighteen grandchildren.

Except in terms of personal prosperity, Joseph tended to do everything on a grand scale; he married three times, presumably partly out of the need to have a partner to look after the children of his first marriage. He lived to the grand old age of 84, his lifetime spanning the long reigns of George II, George III, George IV, and William IV. Within the confines of Cumberland he moved about, it seems, almost endlessly.

Born in the parish of Holme Cultram, near the township of Abbeytown, the third son of John and Martha Huntington, Joseph spent his childhood there, and in 1778, married Charlotte Wilson, a local girl.Their first child, William was born at Abbeytown.in 1779.

By 1781, however, their address was at the neighbouring parish of Bromfield, where the first of three Josephs was baptised, only to die in infancy. By 1785 they had moved right across the county, to Bewcastle, where their second ill-fated Joseph was born, who also died in infancy. Bewcastle was in the isolated border country, north and east of Carlisle, which had been the earlier scene of many border disputes and raids. In 1788, the third Joseph was born, and he was christened at Wigton, along with his twin brother, John.

At that time Joseph Huntington's cousin, Isaac Huntington was recorded in the Wigton Parish Register, as one of the Churchwardens. The family was back in Bromfield, when daughter Martha was christened in 1791, They later returned to Carlisle, where in St.Mary's Church, another pair of twins were baptised in 1794 - Nahamah, and Seth. Whether the choice of these names was due to the influence of the officiating cleric,or to Joseph's foreknowledge that he might run short of names, for his rapidly growing family, is not known. Certainly somebody possessed some imagination at St.Mary's, because a foundling, which had been left in the cloisters, was baptised Mary Abbey. On another occasion, deviating from the usual hum-drum recording of events, it was written "Buried, a man unknown, packed in a box, found at the Coffee House, brought by the Manchester coach, aged 50 (supposed)."

Sadly Nahamah died in the following year. Solomon was baptised on New Year's Day in 1797, across the city at St.Cuthbert's. After bearing ten children since 1779, at least three of them dying in infancy,Charlotte died in September 1797, aged 45, and was buried at St.Cuthbert's.

Joseph lost only a year before he married Mary Graham, of Carlisle, and they only lost a year or so before producing Thomas, who was baptised at St. Cuthbert's, Carlisle, in the spring of 1800.

By 1802 Joseph and his new wife were back in Wigton, where Jonathan and Mary Ann were born. The record of the burial of wife number two, Mary, has not yet been found, but she must have died by 1808, because in 1809, Joseph married his third wife Ruth McCall of Wigton. At that time Ruth was 40, and Joseph was 57 years old. They had just one child, Joseph, who was baptised at Wigton in November 1815. The giving of the name Joseph for the fourth time suggests that the third Joseph, the twin born in 1788, had also died in the interval.

Joseph and Ruth Huntington enjoyed quite a long marriage together despite their late start; Joseph lived until 1836, and Ruth, until 1838, when in her seventieth year. Both were buried at Wigton. Joseph, in his 84 years, had endured his full share of tragedies, particularly, in the loss of several children.

Throughout his life, Joseph was described as a labourer, so he must have found it hard to support his burgeoning family. His constant movement, though , suggests that he was willing to go wherever there was work, and a living to earn. This was a period when there was much enclosure of land; many people who had relied on grazing rights on common land for part of their upkeep, were driven to become labourers; to become employed instead of having at least a measure of independence. It is probable that Joseph was one of these.

The enclosures forced important, but for some, uncomfortable, changes, in the interests of an eventually much more efficient agricultural economy. On the other hand possibly Joseph benefited by being one of the many people employed to carry out the work of enclosing land in Cumberland. In our own time, two hundred years later, most of us are apprehensive about and resistant to, the many changes being wrought by our absorbtion, struggling and screaming all the way, into a larger Europe, with the consequent loss of many traditionally prized customs, rights and privileges.

Many lives were changed by the process of land enclosure, as well as by the development of factory-based weaving and spinning industries, in place of the traditional home-based cottage industries. A migration to the towns was often the inevitable result. In turn the crowded, insanitary conditions to be endured in these towns, whose population increase was not matched by increases in housing stock, led to high rates of mortality. The causes were Typhus, Smallpox, and Cholera. Carlisle, for instance suffered a Typhus outbreak in 1781; and in Whitehaven, 81, mainly children, died from Smallpox in 1772, and 79 in 1776. But Smallpox did not generally spread to the country areas. It was in the towns that the filth caused by overcrowding, ignorance about the need for clean water supplies, and appalling sanitation gave rise to Typhus, Dysentery, and added to the high death rates already suffered, particularly by children, from Scarlet Fever, Whooping Cough, and Diarrhoea.

Not until much later in the eighteenth century were people made sufficiently aware of the remedies necessary to prevent these diseases, and though voices were raised by Robert Rawlinson, of the General Board of Health. For a long time this awareness was not raised to the point where action had to follow. Once this had begun to happen, the newspapers started campaigns for improvements; in 1875 the West Cumberland Times slated the conditions in rural areas; 'At hundreds of farmhouses, the families have no other supply of water than that which is supplied from wells sunk beneath the adjacent manure heaps, the cesspools, and cattlefolds, and piggeries'. With the improvements came dramatic falls, as much as 15%,in the death rates between 1871 and 1890, and the most significant drop was in child mortality. Joseph and Charlotte had lost at least three infants, probably more, because no further mention has been found in the parish registers to mark the survival to adulthood of William, Joanathan or Mary Ann. It is significant that in the following generations of the family, far more of the children born, survived.

In the case of Joseph, it must be remembered that his father, who had become quite prosperous as a weaver, and who died in 1808 at Wigton, had left the bulk of his estate to his youngest daughter Mary, and to her daughter Margaret, (see chapter 6). John's remaining offspring, John, of Sebergham, Martha, who married Robert Potts, Thomas of Arlecdon, and Joseph himself, had had to share equally the residue of his estate after Mary's share. It was probably not very much.

It was common for lowly paid labourers who lived a long time to end up as paupers, living on the charity of the parish. Joseph and Ruth did not suffer that fate, and possibly they, living in Wigton, might have benefitted from the kindness of Joseph's sister Mary, living also at Wigton.

Although Joseph moved about and lived in several places during his lifetime, the town of Wigton was the centre round which his life revolved much of the time. Indeed it was home for several branches of the Huntingtons, and in the adjoining parish of Westward, were several cousinly families. Joseph's father, John had returned to Wigton in his later years, looked after by his daughter Mary. His uncle Joseph's widow, Jane lived on there until she died in 1802, as did their son,(his cousin,) Isaac and his wife Jane.

Wigton, at the turn of the century, had about 2000 inhabitants, a number which rose to about 4000 during the next twenty years, and was a centre for spinning and weaving. The History of Cumberland, published in 1797, gave the number of weavers in the town as about 120, plus a number in adjacent villages. In the previous twenty years, the making of cotton goods had increased rapidly, and Wigton had become one of the leaders of this industry, and was to remain so until machine-equipped factories took the place of mainly cottage industries.

One of the famous sons of Wigton was Dr.John Brown, born in 1715 in Northumberland, who came to Wigton when he was a few months old. He attended the public school at Wigton until he was seventeen, then went to Cambridge, where he gained a Master's Degree. He then became a minor canon at Carlisle,but his subsequent fame arose out of his literary genius. So impressed was the Empress of Russia by his treatise on an educational plan for Russia, that she sent him an invitation to visit her country, together with £1000 to pay for the expenses of his visit - an invitation which he accepted with joy. Unfortunately however, he was the victim of a violent illness, and reluctantly accepted medical advice to cancel his visit. Probably his disappointment, added to his illness, affected the balance of his mind, and in 1766 he took his own life. In addition to having been a celebrated writer and poet of his time, he was also much admired as a musician and a painter. The Biographia Cumbria included, as an example of Dr.Brown's beautiful and elegant prose, his letter to Lord Lyttleton, in which another son of Wigton, Joseph Rook, is described. It ends as follows:

> "But Joseph is contented and happy; and Passing rich with
> less than forty pounds a year."

Of Joseph's offspring who survived childhood, George married Jane Barnes,in 1802, both minors, at St.Cuthbert's Carlisle, and their son William was born in July of the same year, four months after their marriage. William was descibed as a labourer-carting in the 1851 census. He had married Rebecca Kirkup in 1830, and they had three children, Sarah Ann, Jane, and James, in 1832,1833,and 1834 respectively. In 1862 an illegitimate son,William James, was born to Jane. In the 1881 census for Carlisle, Rebecca, then aged 74, a widow, described as a former laundress, was shewn as living at 14 Westmorland Street Carlisle, with John Hoolilen (Hoolahan?) aged 34, shop/tea merchant,and described as Rebecca's son-in-law. His wife Sarah, aged 23, and William James Huntington, aged 18, described as Hoolilen's brother-in-law were also there. The one fact which is sure, is that young William James was the grandson of Rebecca Huntington, and the son of her daughter Jane. Possibly Sarah Ann had married a Hoolilen,and that James Hoolilen was an offspring from that union.

Joseph's son John, the surviving twin, became a weaver, and married Isabella Liovrick at Wigton, in 1808. They produced six children; Mary, Thomas Hornsby (who lived only one year), Charlotte,Henry, George, and Isabella, between 1814 and 1828.

Martha married Christopher Robinson in 1818, and moved to Bromfield. Seth married in 1828, a Rockcliffe girl, Elizabeth Foster, and they had a son Thomas in 1829, after which Elizabeth must have died, because the 1851 Carlisle census shews Seth, a Weaver, married to a Mary, described as a Winder,aged 50.They were living at 172 Queen Street, and nearby at Caldew Side, were living Seth's brother,Solomon, also a weaver, aged 54, with his 61 year old wife Mary. Their step brother, Thomas, aged 51, described as a Plasterer, was living at 45 Crescent Lodge, with his second wife Mary (nee Jackson), aged 48,whom he married in 1847 after his first wife, Isabella, mother of his three children,John,Robert,and Mary, had died in 1846. Of these grandchildren of Joseph Huntington and his wives, we can follow the developments of some of them by means of the 1881 census for Cumberland, always remembering that with the help of the railway systems which had been built since the 1830s, many had migrated to other parts of England, in search of better opportunities. The eldest son of Thomas and Isabella, John, had married Dinah, a Wigton girl,and moved to Maryport. This was a new port and town, which had been founded in the previous century by Humphrey Senhouse, and which he had named after his wife Mary. The town had prospered and had soon attracted new industries. Thomas had become a Lift Engineer at the Ironworks. John and Dinah had five children; Fanny, Thomas Hewitt, Mary, Amy, and Dinah, in the period 1864 to 1879, but Fanny and Thomas Hewitt were missing from the census roll at Maryport in 1881 - possibly they had died young, or maybe they had left home to earn a living elsewhere.

A puzzle arises from the 1881 Carlisle census, in that it names, living at Blackwell Low, Hill Holme Terrace, Henry Huntington, widower, aged 42, occupation, Fitter and Turner, place of birth, Scotforth, Lancashire. With him were living his children,all born in Carlisle; James,15, Elizabeth Ann,11, Isaac,6, and Christopher,4, an earlier Isaac, born in 1860, obviously having died in childhood. The Henry, son of John and Isabella, had been baptised in 1842, but at the time of baptism his age was given as 22, hence his appearance on the tree as having been born in 1820.Whilst it is possible that John and Isabella had, during their career, spent some time in Lancashire, and given birth to Henry, the fact is that Henry's sister Charlotte had been baptised in Wigton, his younger brother George, at Brampton, to the east but near to Carlisle, and the youngest sister, Isabella, at Wigton. It is possible that the Henry in the 1881 Carlisle census was of another branch of Huntingtons, which would mean of course, that James, Elizabeth, Isaac, and Christopher should likewise, not have been shewn on this family tree.On balance, the fact that at the time of Henry's baptism in 1842, his age was given as 22, and his parents named as John and Isabella, indicates that he was our Henry, and that at the time of the 1881 census, his date of baptism '42, was taken erroneously by the enumerator as his age.

George,however, born in Brampton, was recorded as living at Irvin Place, aged

52, (he was baptised in 1823), occupation, General Labourer, with his wife Elizabeth, also 52, and two unmarried children, Henry, a Joiner, aged 30, and a daughter, Mary, aged 19, occupation Gardener/Labourer. Presumably Isabella, born in 1848, had left home, perhaps married, or perhaps had died earlier.

In all, the grandchildren of the prolific Joseph and his wives, were represented by over two dozen grandchildren at the time of the 1881 census in Cumberland. The general increase in population has to be attributed in part to a slowly improving quality of life. Whilst, as has been noted, diseases were still carrying off large numbers of people, particularly infants and young persons, men were marrying younger, thus lengthening their breeding period.

Part of the improved quality of life, though, may have been illusory, because whereas large numbers were moving to the towns to make their living, they were unconsciously taking on the greater dangers to the health of themselves, and their children, by living in the crowded, insanitary conditions then prevalent in those towns.

CHAPTER NINE

THE HUNTINGTONS IN SEBERGHAM

"The Reverend John Stubbs)...is a native of this parish, and does the duties of it much to the satisfaction of the people.... being also the schoolmaster of the village, and a man of very respectable abilities. To him we acknowledge we are indebted...."

Notes from the History of Cumberland, by William Hutchinson, in 1797, referring to the Assistant Curate of The Church of the Virgin Mary, Sebergham, from 1771-1804.

CHART NO.11.
THE SEBERGHAM TREE.

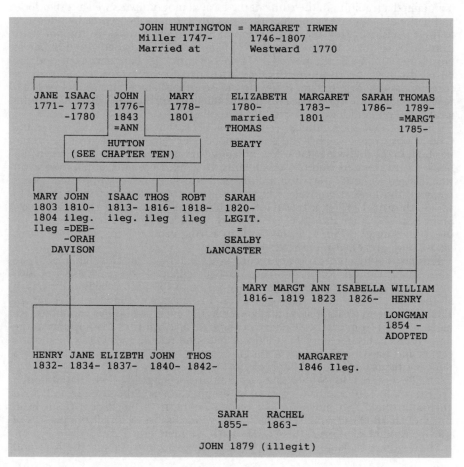

The Solway Plainsmen

Sebergham lies on the Caldew River, about 10 miles South by West of Carlisle, and on the old turnpike road from Penrith to Wigton. Wigton is about 8 miles North by West, so give or take a mile or two, it is more or less equidistant from Carlisle,Penrith, Keswick, and Wigton. It is bounded by the parishes of Dalston, Castle Sowerby, Caldbeck, and Westward. Most of what has been written about Sebergham has praised the village; the Cumberland Directory of 1829 referred to "Sebergham, commonly called 'Church Sebergham' as a charming village, which is generally allowed to be one of the pleasantest in the county." Some references to Sebergham attribute its name to an association with rushes for thatching, these being referred to as "Sieves" by the country people - hence "Sievy-burgh" In the middle of the 18th century, when Burn and Nicolson published their history of Sebergham, the population was estimated at 111 families, all of them Church of England," save one Quaker" In 1791 a count was made, and the houses or families recorded in the village was 140, and "the number of living souls, 736." which was about 5 ½ to a family.

The curates of the Church, which is dedicated to the Virgin Mary, seem to have maintained a tradition in the study of the local demography, as well as other local and national matters. For instance they recorded, from time to time,by reference to their parish register, the relationship of baptisms to burials. In the ten years from 1618 to 1628, they noted that baptisms at 100, exceeded the number of burials by 50, and in the period 1771 to 1781 the 255 baptisms exceeded the burials by 104, the rise in births they attributed to the extensive enclosure of common land in Sebergham, following the Act of Parliament in 1765 its eventual result having been an increase in the productivity of the land. By 1775 all the local common land had been brought into tillage.

The Reverend John Stubbs recorded, in 1771, that the Bell Bridge over the Caldew was swept away by "the greatest flood ever remembered." (A new bridge was built in the following year). A population survey was made in 1782, when 145 houses were counted, and 655 inhabitants. In 1784, December 6th, a frost set in which lasted without interruption until April 5th, 1785.(Note: within the writer's memory, the longest equivalent experience was from December 26th 1962, to about 5th April 1963.) Each year John Stubbs thereby recorded a brief summary of the year's weather, its effect on crops and produce, their market prices, and on the 10th August 1786, " a shock of an earthquake, felt in Northern parts, occasioning great alarm but little damage".

This fascinating contemporary record notes that on 22nd November 1797, he " buried old Duncan Robinson, from Warnell Fell, aged 100 years. He was born in Scotland in 1697, fought for King George 1st in the 1715 rebellion.He was in all the wars, battles, and sieges that Great Britain was engaged in till 1760. In 1766 he came to this parish as a labourer in the enclosure of the commons. He had a pension from Chelsea College of about £6 a year for his sole support in the dreary days of his infirmity. He was intelligent and related with gusto the historic events and hardships of many a rough campaign. He mixed in civil life with a most pacific disposition and benevolence, and died truly loved".

The Reverend John Stubbs gives us as an interesting side note that although the harvest in 1797 was badly spoiled by summer storms, "the grain from Poland got us through". So much for Napoleon's attempts to blockade Britain from Europe! In 1800 he wrote " a horrible war with France, with all the powers of Europe ranged against us, Russia, Denmark, Sweden, etc."

The writings of People like John Stubbs tell us so much about the lives and feelings of his contemporaries, and it is a pity that his enlightening notes came to an end in 1804.

It was frequently the case that incumbent curates held more than one living, in some cases, several livings; many parishes did not provide sufficient income for the curate's perceived needs. It was quite common in such circumstances for the curate to appoint assistant curates, who carried out all the duties of the incumbent on his behalf for a pittance. John Stubbs was such an Assistant Curate, and he supplemented his income by acting as the village teacher, as did many others in his situation. In 1812, it was recorded that, out of ten thousand incumbents, nearly six thousand were non-resident, and Cobbett, in his 'Legacy to Parsons', quoted the'Clerical Guide', showed that 332 parsons shared the revenues of 1496 parishes, and 500 more shared those of 1524 The Reverend John Stubbs had married his bride,Mary Blaylock, in October 1773, at Burgh-by-Sands on the Solway coast of Cumberland and he had the sad task of burying her in July 1794, after she had died giving birth to their ninth child.

Apart from Agriculture, and the occupations which go to support it, there was very little other industry in the village. There were some coal and limepits of long standing nearby, and a bleach- field at Sebergham Bridge. Again the very numerate recorders at Sebergham tell us that the enclosures of previously common land had involved about 4000 acres, and that this addition plus the nearly 3000 acres previously enclosed for cultivation, made a total of about 7000 acres,to be tilled by about 300 persons. This was felt to be quite an efficient standard of cultivation.

John Huntington had been born in Holme Cultram, in 1747, the eldest son of John and Martha Huntington, and we do not know what brought him to Sebergham, but presumably it was to find a job. He married Margaret Irwen in August 1770, at Westward, the parish adjoining Sebergham. There were several Huntingtons in that parish, so he would have had reasons to visit parts of Westward frequently. Presumably Margaret lived in Westward.

The first child born to John and Margaret was Jane, in August 1771. At the baptism, John described himself as a Miller, and it is to be supposed that the mill was situated on the River Caldew. Later on however, John was described as a Labourer, a description used for a wide variety of agricultural duties.

We do not know yet what became of Jane, and so far searches of the local Parish Registers have not revealed anything. It is possible that she died when young, and that this event was overlooked in the records.

The next birth to be recorded was of Isaac on 2nd April 1773, and the address of John and "Peggy" was given as Bridgend Mill. Unhappily Isaac died in November 1780, aged only 7_. Isaac was followed by the author's 3 x great grandfather, John,in January 1776.(See chapter 10). Again the address was given as Bridgend Mill, and the father's occupation was given as Miller.

Mary was born in January 1778, at Bridge End and she lived only 23 years,dying at Castle Sowerby in July 1801. In June 1780,Elizabeth was born,this time John's occupation being given as Labourer, and the address of John and Peggy given as Holme, Sebergham. Elizabeth was destined to have an eventful life, as we shall see later.Another daughter, Margaret, was born in June 1783, but she also died, at the age of 18, just two months after the death of her sister Mary.(At the time of their daughters' deaths in 1801, the address of John and Peggy was given as Southernby, Castle Sowerby. This hamlet is only about 4 miles from Skelton). The next child to be born to John and Peggy was Sarah, in February

1786, of whom we so far have been unable to learn more. Finally, Thomas was born in February 1789, at which time Peggy was 43 years old, having spent 19 years producing and rearing 8 children, and having also played her part in keeping The Reverend John Stubbs busy, both at Church and at School!

SEBERGHAM CHURCH. BOTTOM: BRIDGE END SEBERGHAM

Sebergham

RIGHT:
SEBERG HAM
BRIDGE OVER
CALDEW
RIVER.

LEFT: BELL
BRIDGE
SEBERGHAM

Turning now to the lives of these children, at least three we know had short lives; Isaac, Mary and Margaret; their eldest surviving son became a Joiner/Wheelwright, and went to nearby Skelton, where he married,in 1798, Ann Hutton. Their lives are related in chapter 10, and we shall turn to the others, Thomas, and Elizabeth. Thomas we know, went to Caldbeck, the next parish to the south of Sebergham. His occupation, given in a later census was as a weaver. He married a Margaret, whose maiden name we do not yet know, and who, according to the 1851 census, had been born in Scotland. We also know from that census that she had been born in 1786. In 1851 Thomas's occupation was given as "Barber/Gingham Weaver"

Thomas and Margaret had 5 children,the first four of them their own, and the fifth must have been adopted. Mary was born in 1816, Margaret in 1819, Ann in 1823, and Isabella in 1826. William Henry Longman Huntington was baptised in 1854, when Margaret was 69 years old. It is concluded that Thomas and Margaret adopted William Henry Longman Huntington, probably on the death of both of his parents. Interestingly enough the 1851 census for Caldbeck lists immediately below Thomas and Margaret, and at the same address, Robert Langman, aged 21, and Isabella Langman, aged 22. Robert Langman was recorded as having been born in Cornwall, and his occupation was given as lead miner. With today's knowledge we would rate that as an occupation to be avoided, and it is probable that both these young parents died, and that Thomas and Margaret took William into their family. Little more is known about this family, as they will have grown up at a time when travel was more easy, and therefore they could have moved beyond Cumbria, and the scope of this research. We do know that Ann had an illegitimate daughter, Margaret, at Caldbeck, in December 1846

Returning to Elizabeth, the third daughter of John and Peggy, of Sebergham, born in 1780, the parish register notes that she opened her account in 1803 with the birth of Mary, the first of five illegitimate children, to be born over the ensuing 15 years. The saying goes that one mistake can be bad luck, and that two mistakes shew downright carelessness, but Elizabeth's surely set a record for persistence! At the time of Mary's baptism, Elizabeth's address was given as Limekiln-nook, in neighbouring Castle Sowerby. Sadly Mary lived only 14 weeks until February 1804. John was born in 1810, followed by Isaac in 1813, the address being given as Newlands,Castle Sowerby,. Thomas in 1816, and Robert a year later. No hint is given of the fatherhood, but in 1818 Elizabeth married Thomas Beaty at Sebergham. In 1820 a daughter, Sarah was baptised at Dalston. Her surname was given as Huntington, indicating that she was not the natural daughter of Thomas Beaty. Possibly Sarah was born prior to the marriage in 1818, and baptised when she was two years old.

We know that Sarah married Sealby Lancaster, because they appeared in the 1881 census, in Maryport. Sealby then aged 55 gave his occupation as Cow Keeper, born in Borrowdale, Cumbria, and Sarah was aged 61.Included in their family were a daughter, also Sarah,aged 26, and recorded as unmarried, and another daughter Rachel, aged 18, also unmarried. A child, aged 2,named John Huntington, and described as "Grandson" was the fifth occupant of the house. This requires some puzzling out, and perhaps we shall never know. Finally, the 1851 census for Penrith revealed Elizabeth's son Robert, aged 33, unmarried, and described as a Saddler.

BELOW: LIME KILN NOOK, CASTLE SOWERBY, ELIZABETH'S HOME.
BOTTOM: VIEW FROM CALDBECK COMMON OVER SOLWAY PLAIN TO
CRIFFEL, SCOTLAND.

To return to Sebergham, the register records the burial on 22nd December, 1807, of Peggy Huntington, aged 63. To date it has not been possible to discover when her widower, John Huntington died.

Of Elizabeth's offspring we have not so far accounted for her son John, born in 1810. He married Deborah Davison in 1831, at Castle Sowerby, and they thereafter lived in nearby Caldbeck, where they produced a family comprising Henry, born 1832, Jane, born 1834, Elizabeth in 1837, John in 1840, and finally Thomas in 1842.

In addition to a number of local farmers and yeomen, the 1829 Directory lists a number of residents and their occupations, among which the following feature:

James Armstrong, Victualler String of Horses, Goose Green.

Henry Denton, Gentleman, Green Foot.

Mrs Jane Denton, Green Foot.

John Hall, Grocer

Rev. John Heysham, Sebergham Hall.

Laing, Stone Mason -

William Nicholson, Gentleman, Bridge Cottage.

Stephen Scott, Blacksmith

Edward Bulman, Victualler, Hare Clarke Robson, Bleacher.

Isaac Denton, Surgeon.

Rev. Hugh Elliott, Schoolmaster, and Curate of Highhead.

Henry Hoodless, Joiner, Rattle- David beck.

Elizabeth Rayson, Grocer.

Isaac Richardson, Dancing Master

Wm. Sowerby, Victualler, Kings Arms, Brow Top.

Thomas Barker, Stone Mason, Ewelock hill.

John Gibson, Blacksmith.

William Lamb, Schoolmaster.

Joseph Pugmire, Tailor.

John Simpson, Joiner.

William Simpson, Stone Mason.

John Tiffin, Joiner.

Robert Barnes, Miller, Crookholme Mill.

Rob. Gordon, Shoemaker, Gill Whins

Christopher Moses, Shopkeeper.

Isaac Reed, Vict. & Grocer, The Royal Oak.

John Thompson. Brazier.

John Todd, Schoolmaster.

The list also names about 40 farmers, and Yeomen, and together with these, indicate quite a thriving community, with a good variety of trades and occupations being carried on. Probably this had something to do not only with the fertility of the locality, but also with the fact that Sebergham lay astride a major road between Penrith and Wigton, and almost astride also, another road connecting Keswick and Carlisle, thus broadening the scope for trade. It was noted earlier that, following the destruction in a storm, of the main bridge at Sebergham, no time was lost to build a replacement - no Town and Country Planning Act to slow down developments then! It is interesting to note that David Laing, Stonemason, mentioned in the 1829 Directory, was the father of James Laing (1817-82), the founder of the famous international construction company which carries the name of John Laing PLC. James Laing started by building a number of houses in Sebergham, using local sandstone, and cobbles from the river Caldew.

It is interesting to find out how much people were paid by their employers at the time of this story. We are fortunate in that a number of prominent citizens in Cumbria kept meticulous records, and that many of these have been preserved. Among these were the Senhouse records, and for example, in 1770 he noted the following wages paid:

To Ned, his ½ year's wage	£4/10/-. (£4.50pence)
To Mary her ½ year's wage	£3.
To Jno. his Martinmas wage	£2.
To Betty her ½ year's wage	£2/5/-. (£2.25pence)

Many others were paid on a piece-work basis, or a rate per day, thus:

Mowing and making Hay,	18d. or 19d per day (7 ½ pence or 8p)
Making Hay (women and youths)	9 ½d to 13_d per day (4 pence to 6p)
Masons	1s10d per day (9p)

Over the ensuing years wages improved somewhat, but their levels were prone to fluctuation, according to economic circumstances. Thus, as late as 1841, at the end of the period of this story, a petition was sent by the Mayor and Aldermen of Carlisle to the House of Commons, reporting that there were 1465 people in that city earning no more than 1/- (5 pence) a week; 1623 earning between 1/- and 1/6d (7 ½p) a week; 692 earning between 1/6d and 2/- (10 Pence) a week, and 635 between 2/- and 3/- (15 pence) per week; in all, nearly 6000 in that city alone, averaging only 1/2d (6 pence) per week. These were of course the 'Hungry Forties' when trade was depressed, and the repeal of the Corn Laws was still some years away, but it is indicative of how perilously so many people had to live. The same petition reported that up to a 1000 persons in Carlisle were dependant on 'casual charity'.

RIGHT: CALDBECK

BELOW:ST. MUNGO'S
CHURCH, CALDBECK.
.

The research required to identify the events in Family History requires a patient study of numerous Parish records. It is impossible to do this without realising that, in Cumberland and Westmorland at least, there was a high level of illegitimacies. In addition, the same research reveals also a very high level of what must have been 'shotgun marriages'. These are subjects about which very little reference has been made in most studies of social history. Although we, in the twentieth century, may think of ourselves as being fairly liberal in these matters, the fact remains that most of us have inherited from the Victorian generations, many of their social mores, albeit unconsciously. Whatever the case, we tend to view the behaviour of our earlier predecessors through a mental lens distorted by those mores. The pre-Victorians seem to have had a much more relaxed view about pre-marital sex and about illegitimate births, especially if these led to a marriage. The curate might frown on such behaviour, but generally the uppermost concern seems to have been that bastards, and their mothers, should not become a burden to be supported out of parish funds.

In Cumberland, in the nineteenth century, the proportion of illegitimate births was of the order of 120-140 bastards to each 1000 births, according to Dr.J.D.Marshall, in his book 'The Lake Counties from 1830 to the mid-Twentieth century', written jointly with John K.Walton. He went on to note that Cumberland and Westmorland produced bastardy rates some 80% above those obtaining for England as a whole. He noted two striking similarities between Cumberland and Scotland, the one being the good news that both held a high value for education, the result being good educational standards; the other was the bad news that Cumberland shared with Scotland the doubtful honour of having high illegitimacy rates.

Various possible reasons have been put forward for this latter phenomenon. It is a recorded fact that marriages tended to occur later in life, largely for economic reasons, and that the resultant strains were a cause. Again, Dr. Marshall has pointed out that in the mid-nineteenth century, the proportion of unmarried women in Cumberland was of the order of 32-34%, against the national average of 28%. Others have blamed the trend on simpler factors, such as the 'immodest' arrangements in farmhouses, which threw men and women servants together. Yet others have suggested that the common factors between Scots and Cumbrians, of high literacy and high illegitimacy rates were in some way connected as regional peculiarities, because they provided a basis for personal ambition on the one hand, and they represented a symptom of strain and frustration within individual lives and within families, on the other.

What of Birth Control practices? Here again the facts are largely shrouded by a curtain of silence on the subject, and it is more than likely that many young country people were fairly ignorant on this matter. Nevertheless, whilst within many marriages, the spacing out ,or rather the non-spacing out of births indicates that little or no birth control, apart possibly from abstinence, was practiced, there were equally numerous instances where families had obviously been planned. The most obvious methods of controlling births would have been either by prolonging the nursing of infants - a method within the power of the mothers, or by using the 'withdrawal' method - coitus interruptus - a risky method which depended upon the forbearance of the male. Other methods known were crude forms of 'barriers', either oils or some sort of fabric, intended to frustrate the sperm, but it is not known whether these methods would have been known to the country people; in any case these methods were certainly not sure ones To quote Eve Mclaughlin on the subject, 'The betrothed couple enjoyed most of the privileges of the married couple, and if the girl became pregnant, all was well so long as the bride made it up the church steps before she went into labour.'

The general attitude to this whole subject is perhaps best illustrated by the following report, extracted from the Carlisle Journal, in January 1869:

"Night Courting.- The Royal Commissioners who have been considering the laws of marriage had some evidence on the subject of courtship and matrimony in Scotland. A medical man of forty years experience informed the commissioners that among the agricultural working classes the ordinary time for courtship is the middle of the night. Farm servants get out of the house when everybody else is in bed, go to a neighbouring farmhouse, and rouse a young woman in it by making a noise at her window. The girl comes to the window, and if she knows the young man, or after a little parley,if she does not know him, she either admits him into her bedroom, or comes out and goes with him into an out-house for courting. There is no courtship in any other form. The fathers and mothers will not allow their daughters to meet a young man in the daytime, and the young man never visits the family; but the parents quite allow this. They have done it themselves before. If the father knows it is going on he lies comfortably in his bed, just as a father in a higher rank of life would shut his eyes to his daughter going out for a walk with a young man. This medical witness says that he has remonstrated with parents when ill consequences have followed, but they say that their daughters must have husbands and there is no other way of courting. The young man visits the girl in this way probably once a week. Marriage very commonly follows in case of need. Relatives interfere when they find the case requires it, and then, if possible, marriage is hurried on. If the young man is well-behaved, and the young woman is at all respectable, she insists on being married, or the connection is dropped; but young men who have no particular tie to the neighbourhood, and can go easily away to another farm service, very often abandon the girl, and leave the place.. Marriage follows, perhaps in two thirds of the cases, and frequently the expectation of thus securing a husband leads a young woman more easily to fall. The witness states that in attending midwifery cases among the working classes he notices that it is very rare to find that the first child born so long as eight months after marriage. The general feeling among these classes is that is that if they are afterwards married, and any previous offspring thus legitamised, there has been no sin, as in fact there was no scandal, no shame, no disgrace."

Dr. John Marshall, Reader Emeritus in Regional History at the University of Lancaster, has added the comment on Cumbrian Communities that historically they had very low crime rates, but that they did encourage 'night courting', which led to the large number of pregnant brides.

VIEWS FROM CALDBECK COMMON: TOP,LOOKING NORTH OVER
SOLWAY,BOTTOM: LOOKING SOUTH TO THE CALDBECK FELLS.
REPRODUCED BY KINDNESS OF MR. WILSON SWAN.

Sebergham

CHART NO.12
ANOTHER HUNTINGTON FAMILY IN SEBERGHAM

```
JOHN HUNTINGTON 1721-1808 AND MARTHA SKELTON 1715-1788
BORN AT THURSBY                  BORN AT HOLME CULTRAM
                    PARENTS OF
  MARTHA   JOHN   WILLIAM   JOSEPH      THOMAS   MARY
  1745-    1747-  1749-     1752-1836   1755-    1757-1840
           SEE 1STPAGE                  =MARTHA
           OF THIS CHAPTER              BOWMAN

JOHN= (1)JULIA KIRKER D.1816   WILLIAM SKELTON THOMAS ANTHONY
      (2)MARY ROUTLEDGE              SEE ARLECDON CHAPTER

THE FAMILY OF JOHN, JULIA AND MARY HUNTINGTON IN SEBERGHAM
-----------------------------------------------------------

                JOHN HUNTINGTON  = (1) JULIA KIRKER
                BORN LOWESWATER  |    M.1815 D.1816
                1785-            | (2) MARY ROUTLEDGE
                                   BORN CARLISLE M.1818

(1)      (2)    (2)     (2)     (2)     (2)    (2)   (2)     (2)    (2)   (2
JULIA  JANE  THOMAS  MARY  SKELTON   ISA-  JOHN  ANTH- JAMES WM.ISAAC
1816-  1821- 1821-   ANN   1824-     BELLA 1830- ONY        1837 '41
=      =             1822- =         1826- =     1835-  =          =
JOS.   THOS          ANN             ANN   1920  ELIZB.  MARY
HETH-  DIXON         HETHER-               MARY
ERING               INGTON                 ANN
-TON                SEE NEXT PAGE          PURDOM  ANNIE
                                           1840-   1857-
                                           1912

                THOMAS   MARY-ANN  ELIZABETH     ISABELLA  JOHN
                1852-    1854-     1858-         BOTH 1874 GEORGE


JOHN   MARY-ANN  ANNE   ANTHONY  ELIZABT  ISABELLA  SKELTON  DAVID
1857-  1860-     1863-  1865-    1868-    1870-     1872-    PURDOM
                        1937                                 1875-
                        =JANE REED
                        -1865-1922

JOHN     WILLIAM   ERNEST     JANE     GEORGE      EDMUND   MARY   SARAH
1887-    REED                 REED     JAMES                HILDA  USHER
1939     1890-1966 1893-1965  1895-    1897-1974   1900-67  1903-  1906-
=EMMA                         1945
CHANDLER
1884-1954

JANE AINSWORTH 1914-1991*ERNEST 1915-80*MARY REED1918*JOHN1923-44
=THOMAS JOHN PHILLIPS
ISSUE: PAUL J.PHILLIPS
```

SOME DESCENDANTS OF SKELTON
AND ANN HUNTINGTON
CHART NO.13

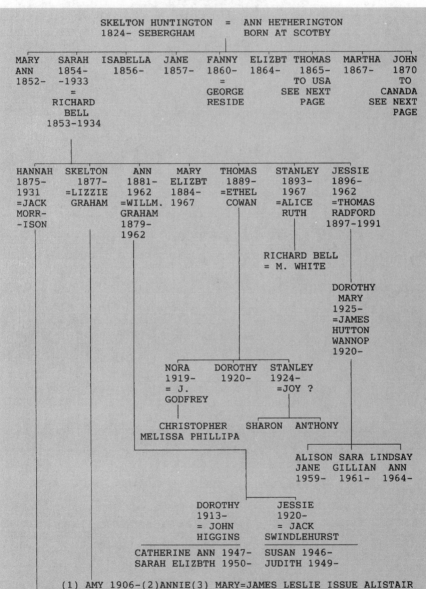

```
            SKELTON HUNTINGTON  =  ANN HETHERINGTON
            1824- SEBERGHAM        BORN AT SCOTBY

MARY    SARAH  ISABELLA  JANE    FANNY  ELIZBT  THOMAS  MARTHA  JOHN
ANN     1854-  1856-     1857-   1860-  1864-   1865-   1867-   1870
1852-   -1933                    =              TO USA          TO
        =                        GEORGE         SEE NEXT        CANADA
        RICHARD                  RESIDE         PAGE            SEE NEXT
        BELL                                                    PAGE
        1853-1934


HANNAH  SKELTON   ANN      MARY     THOMAS   STANLEY   JESSIE
1875-   1877-     1881-    ELIZBT   1889-    1893-     1896-
1931    =LIZZIE   1962     =ETHEL   =ETHEL   1967      1962
=JACK   GRAHAM    =WILLM.  1967     COWAN    =ALICE    =THOMAS
MORR-             GRAHAM                     RUTH      RADFORD
-ISON            1879-                                 1897-1991
                 1962
                                            RICHARD BELL
                                            = M. WHITE

                                                     DOROTHY
                                                     MARY
                                                     1925-
                                                     =JAMES
                                                     HUTTON
                                                     WANNOP
                                                     1920-

                     NORA     DOROTHY  STANLEY
                     1919-    1920-    1924-
                     = J.              =JOY ?
                     GODFREY

                     CHRISTOPHER  SHARON  ANTHONY
                     MELISSA PHILLIPA

                                     ALISON SARA LINDSAY
                                     JANE   GILLIAN ANN
                                     1959-  1961-  1964-

                     DOROTHY        JESSIE
                     1913-          1920-
                     = JOHN         = JACK
                     HIGGINS        SWINDLEHURST

                CATHERINE ANN 1947-   SUSAN 1946-
                SARAH ELIZBTH 1950-   JUDITH 1949-

        (1) AMY 1906-(2)ANNIE(3) MARY=JAMES LESLIE ISSUE ALISTAIR
(1)FRED1902-90=DORA LAMB:       (2):ANNIE1905-35=ANTHONY GEM .
DAUGHTER FREDA 1926-                 DAUGHTER NANCY 1931-
```

DESCENDANTS IN NORTH AMERICA OF THOMAS HUNTINGTON (1865-1936)- CHART NO.14

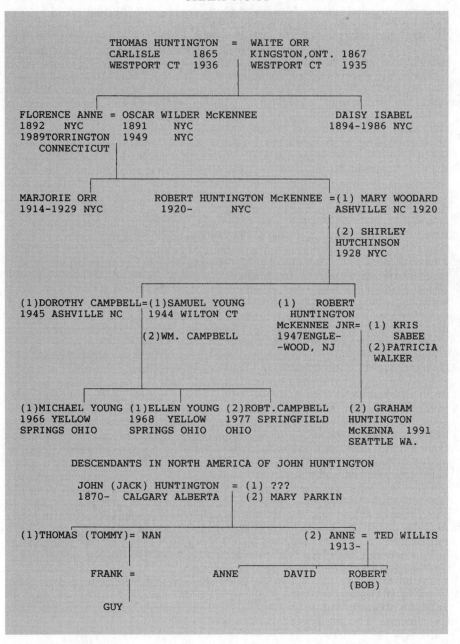

```
                    THOMAS HUNTINGTON  =  WAITE ORR
                    CARLISLE      1865    KINGSTON,ONT. 1867
                    WESTPORT CT   1936    WESTPORT CT    1935


FLORENCE ANNE = OSCAR WILDER McKENNEE              DAISY ISABEL
1892    NYC     1891    NYC                        1894-1986 NYC
1989TORRINGTON  1949    NYC
CONNECTICUT


MARJORIE ORR           ROBERT HUNTINGTON McKENNEE =(1) MARY WOODARD
1914-1929 NYC              1920-       NYC             ASHVILLE NC 1920

                                                  (2) SHIRLEY
                                                      HUTCHINSON
                                                      1928 NYC


(1)DOROTHY CAMPBELL=(1)SAMUEL YOUNG      (1)   ROBERT
1945 ASHVILLE NC    1944 WILTON CT             HUNTINGTON
                                              McKENNEE JNR= (1) KRIS
                   (2)WM. CAMPBELL       1947ENGLE-          SABEE
                                         -WOOD, NJ      (2)PATRICIA
                                                           WALKER


(1)MICHAEL YOUNG (1)ELLEN YOUNG (2)ROBT.CAMPBELL   (2) GRAHAM
1966 YELLOW       1968 YELLOW    1977 SPRINGFIELD   McKENNA  1991
SPRINGS OHIO      SPRINGS OHIO   OHIO               SEATTLE WA.

        DESCENDANTS IN NORTH AMERICA OF JOHN HUNTINGTON

        JOHN (JACK) HUNTINGTON  = (1) ???
        1870-  CALGARY ALBERTA    (2) MARY PARKIN


(1)THOMAS (TOMMY)= NAN                    (2) ANNE = TED WILLIS
                                              1913-

        FRANK =            ANNE        DAVID      ROBERT
                                                  (BOB)

        GUY
```

Soon after the family of John and Peggy Huntington had grown up, John's nephew, also named John, the eldest son of Thomas and Martha,(see chapter 7), moved to the village with his wife, Mary,(nee Routledge). The common ancestors of these two John Huntingtons, were John and Martha Huntington, of Holme Cultram, they being uncle and nephew respectively.

When John married Mary Routledge in May 1818 at St. Cuthbert's Church in Carlisle, he was described as a widower. More research revealed that he had indeed married, at the same church, Julia Kirker, in June 1815. That marriage had been witnessed by Margaret Huntington. It is most likely that the Margaret who played witness to the marriage was his cousin, the illegitimate (and evidently much-loved) daughter of Mary Huntington, who had been born in 1792 at Holme Cultram, at the home of her grandfather John Huntington. The bride, Julia, died in childbirth aged 21, and was buried at St.Cuthbert's, Carlisle in April 1816. Her daughter, Julia Martha, lived, and later married Joseph Hetherington.

The newly married John and Mary Huntington moved to Sebergham, where they lived at Gill Whins, and in April 1821,baptised two children, Jane and Thomas. So far Thomas has not been traced, but we know that Jane married Thomas Dixon at Wigton, in September, 1844. Next, in April 1822, came Mary Ann, and it was noted in the register that John was a Labourer. Skelton was baptised in November 1824, and Isabella, in October 1826. No mention can subsequently be found of Isabella, but Skelton married Ann Hetherington, in Scotland, and after spending some years in Northumberland, where their first four daughters, Mary Ann (1852), Sarah (1854) Isabella (1856), and Jane, (1857, were born. they settled in Carlisle, where five more children, Fanny (1860),Elizabeth (1864), Thomas (1865), Martha (1867), and John (1870), were born, being baptised at Christchurch, Carlisle. Thomas subsequently emigrated to the U.S.A., and his younger brother, John, later emigrated to Canada. The descendants, in North America, of Thomas and John, (Jack) Huntington, are shown on a tree at the end of this chapter, where, also some more notes are given.

Fanny Huntington married George Reside, of Carlisle, in 1884. George had been employed on the Railway, and later became an Engine Driver.

To continue with the children of John and Mary, the next baptisms were of three children on the same day in 1835; John, who had been born in 1830, James, born some time between John and Anthony, who had been born in 1835.The address given at the time of the baptism was Thwaites, a tiny hamlet half a mile west of the village of Sebergham, near the crossroads of the Wigton-Penrith, and the Carlisle-Keswick roads. All three survived infancy, John to marry an Ann, to live at Highhead, and to produce a family - Thomas,in 1852, Mary Ann,in 1854, and, back at Gill Whins, Sebergham, Elizabeth, in 1858. In the register, John was described as a Husbandman. John's brother, Anthony married Mary Ann Purdom, and they had a family comprising John born in 1857, and the following seven, born in Carlisle:Mary Ann, in 1860, Anne in 1863, Anthony in 1865, Elizabeth in 1868, Isabella in 1870, Skelton in 1872, and David Purdom, in 1875. James married an Elizabeth, and they had one child Annie born at Sebergham in 1857. Further children, not recorded by the International Genealogical Index, may have been born later..

The next to arrive was William, in 1837, of whom no further trace has yet been found.In 1841 Isaac was born. He married a Mary,(surname unknown), and in 1874,she presented him with Isabella and John George,both being baptised on the same day. The family lived at Beaumont.

Sebergham

To sum up, John and Mary produced a family of ten children and so far as we can tell with available information, all survived infancy. These in turn produced nineteen children, so that branch certainly proved prolific. A great deal of further research would be necessary to track the fortunes of these offspring, because the major source of family information, beyond that personally handed on, is the International Genealogical Index. For Cumbria the completeness of this source is extremely high until the mid- nineteenth century, largely because centrally kept records have been kept since 1837, and this was considered to be sufficient to take the place of the IGI.

BELOW: ALL THAT REMAINS OF GILL WHINS AT SEBERGHAM.

ABOVE: THWAITES, NEAR SEBERGHAM, WHERE JOHN, JAMES AND
ANTHONY WERE BORN

The span of this chapter on Sebergham covers roughly about sixty years,
during which the Agricultural Revolution had begun in earnest. This revolution
was largely demand-led by the explosion of population in England which grew
from about 5 million in 1750, to 10 million by 1810. As can be seen, the
Huntingtons in Sebergham, as well asother parishes, made their contribution
toward this growth.

The Land Enclosures referred to earlier in this chapter helped make this
growth in agricultural output possible,though the policy brought about many
hardships, particularly for the smaller farmers and yeomen. In many instances,
especially in the nineteenth century, the enclosures took place following an Act
of parliament, of which the commoners and others about to be deprived of their
land, had no advance warning. Thus, even if they had had the knowledge and
the means to do so, they had no chance to challenge the enclosure.Even had they
managed to save their rights pertaining to the land in question, most of them
could not afford the expenses of ditching and hedging. Many cottagers and small
land holders lost their grazing rights on formerly common land, causing them to
become labourers. Many more drifted to the towns, where jobs were being
created by the Industrial Revolution, then in full swing.

Although in theory these people had rights to challenge the Acts which led to
enclosure, in fact these rights to the small men were illusory, for as has been
pointed out above, often the Acts were passed by Parliament without their prior
knowledge. Any challenges to their enforcement were considered by
Commissioners from the very class of large landholders who stood to gain from

the proposed enclosures.

The attitude of most of the 'landed class' was summed up by Lord Sheffield, in the course of one of the debates in Parliament. He described the commoners as a nuisance, and Mr John Billinsley, who wrote the Report on Somerset for the Board of Agriculture in 1795, described in some detail the enervating atmosphere of the commoners' life. 'Besides', he wrote, 'moral effects of an injurious tendency accrue to the cottager, from a reliance on the imaginary benefits of stocking a common. The possession of a cow or two, with a hog, and a few geese, naturally exalts the peasant in his own conception, above his brethren in the same rank of society. It inspires some degree of confidence in a property inadequate to his support. In sauntering after his cattle, he acquires a habit of indolence. Quarter, half, and occasionally whole days are imperceptibly lost. Day labour becomes disgusting, the aversion increases by indulgence; and at length the sale of a half-fed calf or hog furnishes the means of adding intemperance to idleness'

Another, a Mr. Bishton, who wrote the report on Shropshire in 1794, gives a still more interesting glimpse into the mind of the enclosing class: 'The use of common land by labourers operates on the mind as a sort of independence'. When common lands are enclosed, 'the labourers work every day in the year, their children will be put out to labour early', and 'that subordination of the lower ranks of society, which in present times is so much wanted, would thereby be considerably secured.'

The Agricultural Revolution was also greatly aided by many innovations and inventions which helped to increase agricultural efficiency. Jethro Tull's machine drill for sowing facilitated sowing by rows instead of broadcast sowing. This made crop protection from weeds easier to achieve. The waste of fallow land was reduced by Charles Townshend's pioneering of Crop Rotation. He also improved soil fertilisation and drainage practices. Thomas Coke made a valuable contribution to land improvement by better land manuring methods. Robert Bakewell introduced a new breed of sheep, raising the quality and yield of wool. the writings of Arthur Young, and his tours of the country, spread the awareness of these better methods. Greater efficiency needed larger farms, and, following the Enclosure Act, this need was fulfilled, albeit at the cost of squeezing out many small farmers. In the period 1770-1800, the price of land rose sixfold, and this gave the impetus to that squeezing out of the small man.On the international scene, the period saw England involved in the American War of Independence, and this inevitably had its effect on trade. Later in the period, as we have seen from the comments of the Reverend John Stubbs, the Napoleonic wars caused much concern, even in far-away Cumbria. In between his notes for 1797, mostly referring to the weather and crop yields, he remarks " The war with France still rages, and there has been alarm after alarm of threatened invasion"

With the end of that war in 1815, the Industrial Revolution grew apace, though at that time Britain's economy was still mainly agricultural. With this revolution came vast improvements in travel possibilities, and from about 1840 onwards, populations were scattered over the country, making it not quite so easy to research the happenings to what had been,in Cumbria at least,a fairly static scene.

As a postscript, since the drafting of this chapter began letters have been received from other descendants of Skelton and Ann Huntington, among them one from Mrs Dorothy Wannop, of Dalston, near Carlisle. She is the grand-daughter of Sarah Huntington, born in 1854, who married Richard Bell, a Carpenter, of Carlisle, and Dorothy has kindly sent a photograph of her grandparents, taken at a guess, about 1905. Their descendants have been duly entered on the chart no.13.

BELOW:SARAH (NEE HUNTINGTON 1854-1933),& RICHARD BELL (1853-1934) SARAH WAS A DAUGHTER OF SKELTON & ANN HUNTINGTON NEE HETHERINGTON

It is interesting to note the occupations of these later generations, descendants as they were, from weavers, (John and Martha), a carpenter, (Thomas), labourer,(John), Domestic servant,(Skelton),and the daughters most usually also in domestic service. In contrast, the careers open to these later generations provided much wider horizons, and for instance, the 1881 census records that Skelton's children had a variety of occupations; Fanny being a dressmaker, Elizabeth being a bookbinder, Thomas was a coach-builder, the younger ones being scholars

Of Sarah's children Hannah worked at Carrick's Hattery, Ann worked in an office at Robinson Brothers, Mary owned a dressmaking business, Thomas at one time was a partner in a furniture shop. Later he was a salesman. Stanley was a warehouseman, and the youngest sibling, Jessie was a milliner. This illustrates how greatly the dependence of Cumbrians on farming and related trades had changed very rapidly from about 1820.

As indicated above, Jack Huntington married twice; his first wife died from the effects of gas whilst undergoing dentistry, leaving a son Tommy. Jack then married Mary Parkin, a Scotsby girl, and the small family migrated to Calgary, Alberta, where their daughter Anne was born, in 1913. Tommy Huntington, who is now in his nineties, married Pamela Schneider, and they produced a son named Guy. Anne Huntington became a 'war bride' but in reverse from the usual pattern; she met and married Ted Willis, an Englishman serving in the Royal Air Force. He brought Anne back to England, where, after the war he joined the BBC, his career being that of Journalist.

RIGHT: BOB WILLIS
CRICKETER,
WARWICKSHIRE AND
ENGLAND CAPTAIN.

The Solway Plainsmen

Anne Willis relates that her husband Ted was sometimes taken to be the Ted Willis (later Lord Willis) who has entertained millions with his plays and situation comedies on television. Anne and Ted's real and unchallengeable claim to fame is that after their first two children, Anne and David, came Bob Willis, who grew up to become a famous cricketer; in whose time, and under whose captaincy, England regained the 'Ashes' from Australia. Bob was England's fast bowler, and in his Test career, he claimed 325 test wickets, for an average of 25.2 runs - amongst English players, a total only exceeded by Ian Botham. 128 of those batsmen dismissed were Australians, and his best performance in an innings was eight wickets for the cost of 43 runs, at Leeds against the Australians Today, retired from first class cricket, his is a familiar face as a cricket commentator on TV screens; whilst this is being written, he is broadcasting from Sydney, and reporting on the third test match where, England already two matches down, are busy losing the series in a spectacular manner.

Thomas Huntington, (1865-1936), the elder son of Skelton and Ann Huntington, (and the elder brother of Jack who had emigrated to Canada) emigrated to New York as a coach builder, working for the Anderson Company in Manhattan. There he married Waite Orr, a seamstress from Kingston, Ontario, Canada. Later Thomas went to work for Rolls Royce in Long Island, building the wooden portions of their automobile bodies. Thomas retired from there in 1930, and moved to Westport in Connecticut, (about 50 miles north of New York City. With him he took Daisy Isabel (1894-1986), the younger of his two daughters, who never married. They wished to live near to the family of Thomas' elder daughter, Florence Anne (1892-1989). She had married Oscar Wilder McKennee, and lived at Westport, Connecticut. They had two children, Marjorie Orr, who died in 1929 at the age of only 15, and Robert Huntington McKennee.

After Oscar died, the widow Florence and her sister Daisy lived out their lives together at 40 West 55th Street in Manhattan, both living well into their nineties.

Robert Huntington McKennee's career was in advertising, and now he has retired to Washington Depot in Connecticut, with his second wife, Shirley. His daughter Dorothy Campbell (Cam), was born in North Carolina in 1945, where her father, Robert Huntington McKennee, was serving in the U.S. Army Air Force. She had married firstly, Sam Young, and later, in 1972, William Campbell. Dorothy has three children, Michael Young, born in 1966, at Yellow Springs, Ohio, Ellen Young, born in 1968, and Robert Campbell, born in 1977, at Springfield, Ohio.

Robert Huntington McKennee's son, also named Robert Huntington McKennee, Junior, was born in 1947 at Englewood, New Jersey, and he is married to Patricia (nee Walker), and they have a son, Graham Huntington McKennee, born in 1991 at Seattle. They now live in Mill Valley, near San Francisco, California. Michael Young is currently on a teaching fellowship at Brown University, Providence, Rhode Island, working on a Ph.D. in philosophy, and Ellen Young is an elementary schoolteacher in Northeast Harbor, Maine. So the Huntington clan whose roots stem from Cumbria thrives in the New World, and one notes that the habit of longevity appears tenaciously over there also!

LEFT: CALGARY ALBERTA
C.1917 JACK
HUNTINGTON & MARY
(PARKIN)
TOMMY HUNTINGTON
AND ANNE HUNTINGTON
(WILLIS)

RIGHT: TOMMY
HUNTINGTON SERVING IN
CANADIAN ARMY DURING
W.W.2.

CHAPTER TEN

HUNTINGTONS IN SKELTON

"The memory of man passeth away as the remembrance of a guest that tarried but one day". (Wisdom of Solomon).

Inscription in the Skelton Parish Register made in 1788 by the incoming curate, the Reverend John Wilson..

CHART NO.15
THE SKELTON TREE

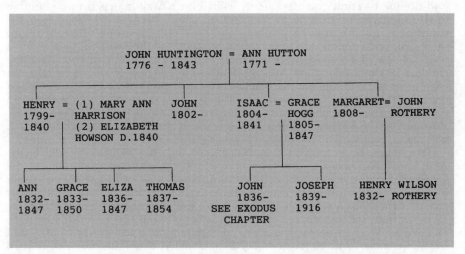

```
                    JOHN HUNTINGTON = ANN HUTTON
                    1776 - 1843     │ 1771 -

 ┌──────────────────┬──────┴──────────┬──────────────┬───────────┐
 HENRY = (1) MARY ANN   JOHN      ISAAC = GRACE   MARGARET= JOHN
 1799-   HARRISON       1802-     1804-   HOGG     1808-    ROTHERY
 1840    (2) ELIZABETH            1841    1805-
         HOWSON D.1840                    1847

 ┌─────┬──────┬──────┬──────┐     ┌──────────┬──────────┬──────────────┐
 ANN   GRACE  ELIZA  THOMAS       JOHN       JOSEPH     HENRY WILSON
 1832- 1833-  1836-  1837-        1836-      1839-      1832- ROTHERY
 1847  1850   1847   1854         SEE EXODUS 1916
                                  CHAPTER
```

A branch of the family was founded in Skelton at the beginning of the nineteenth century, by the marriage of John Huntington, from Sebergham, and Ann Hutton who had been baptised on the 25th July 1771, at St. Michael's Church, Skelton. Her father, Henry Hutton was described in the parish register as 'of Allonby'. There is a village called Allonby on the west coast of Cumbria, west of Aspatria. However, there is also a hamlet called Ellonby about 2 miles west of Skelton, and it is thought to be much more likely that Henry Hutton was 'of Ellonby'. Henry Hutton died at the age of 42, on December 20th, 1779, when Ann was eight years old. He had only outlived, by 14 months, his father, Jonathan Hutton, who died, aged 82, on September 25th 1778. So there is little doubt that the Huttons were local to Skelton, as all these events were recorded there.

The village of Skelton lies about 6 miles north-west of Penrith close to the road from that town to Wigton. It was described in a local Directory in 1829 as " a neat compact village, pleasantly seated on an eminence 6 miles NW of Penrith" The parish school had been built in 1750 by Mr Isaac Milner, and in 1817 was endowed by the Reverend Nelson with £1000. This was used to purchase

£1078.5.5d of 3% Consols, which yielded an income of £32.6.10d., used to pay the Master for teaching 28 free-scholars.

A treasured possession in the Huntington family is the hand-written exercise book, in the writing of Isaac Huntington, which details a wide range of practical subjects which he had been taught at the school. The school still exists, though in a different location in Skelton, and is now managed by Mr.Graham Morley. In the mid- 1980s the school took part in gathering information about Skelton for the 20th century Doomsday Survey, now stored by the BBC on their Domesday Disk.

A study of the parish registers of Cumberland, and particularly the records of marriages, brings home the comparatively large numbers of people who could sign their names. Even though this might have been the extent of the literacy for many of them, it at very least highlights a wish or a tendency for them to acquire some learning. Dr. J.D.Marshall, in his "The Lake Counties from 1830 to the mid-twentieth century, written jointly with John K.Walton, has drawn attention to the similarity of attitude to educational values, between the Scots and the Cumbrians. In both cases large numbers of rural parents strongly desired to give their children enough education to enable them, if they wished, to aim for a wider choice of occupations. As a result basic schooling was provided for the children of Cumberland and Westmorland more extensively and earlier than in most other parts of England. Not only were the towns provided with schools and teachers, but many schools were established in rural settings, and Skelton is a typical example. The school exercise book referred to, includes exercises in basic mathematics, as well as training in the work of artificers, such as bricklaying, plastering, roofing, joinery, masonry, glazing, and even very basic accounting.

Here again, Dr Marshall has drawn attention to the statistics offered in the Abstracts of Marriages in the Reports of the Registrar-General, setting out the levels of alphabetism, as indicated by the numbers who had signed their names in the marriage certificates, over the periods 1855-9, and 1872-6, in primarily rural districts. For a selection of districts in Cumberland and Westmorland, for these periods, the percentage of males was 90.4% and 92.4%, and for females, 80.5% and 89.2%, whereas the mean for England as a whole were 72.0% and 82.4% for males, and 60.9% and 75.7% for females. The Education Act of 1870 was too recent to have had much effect on the figures for 1872- 6.

The population of Skelton at the beginning of this story was 270 (1801), and twenty years later, 1821, the population had risen to 332, so it was rising quite steadily, at about one per cent each year. In addition to a number of local farmers, the 1829 Directory lists the following persons, and their occupations:

The Reverend Tovey Jolliffe B.D. Rector
The Reverend George Allen, Curate.
The Reverend Joseph Barnes, Curate of Hutton

Mrs. Mary Bowbank	William Dobson, Tailor
Mrs. Catherine Fenton	George Forster, Blacksmith
William Graham, Farrier.	John Hartness, Joiner & Wheelwt
Richard Hogg, Parish Clerk and	John Huntington, Joiner and
Victualler, "Weary Sportsman"	Wheelwright
Thomas Loraine, Schoolmaster.	Joseph Nelson, Gardener.
John Pickering, Cooper.	William Tinkler, shopkeeper.
John Warwick, Victualler	Thomas Wetherell, Shoemaker.
"The Salutation"	William Whitelock, Shopkeeper.

The above list probably represented a typical list of occupations for a self-contained community within reasonable distance of the amenities of a fairly large town. Noticeably absent from the list are Doctors, ... and Undertakers, though possibly the Joiners fulfilled some of the latter's duties! The 1829 Directory lists a number of persons in Skelton, whose lives were intertwined with the Huntingtons. John Huntington is listed as a Joiner and Wheelwright, as are Joseph Grindal, a successful local farmer, Richard Hogg, Parish Clerk and licensee of the 'Weary Sportsman', one of whose daughters, Grace, married Isaac Huntington, thus, together with his wife Mary, qualified to become Great-great-great-Grandparents of the author.

Listed at nearby Riggdyke were the Howsons, one of whose daughters, Elizabeth, was to marry John Huntington's eldest son, Henry, whilst another Howson was to become apprenticed in the Joinery business, and eventually to take it over after the Huntingtons of Skelton had died.

When she was 20 years old, Ann Hutton gave birth to an illegitimate daughter, baptised Catherine on June 27th 1792, at Skelton. The parish register did not record the name of the father, and so we are left to puzzle that out.

John Huntington married Ann at Skelton on 12th April 1798, his age being given as 22 and Ann's as 26. They were married by licence, a normal thing as John was from another parish. It is thought unlikely that John was the natural father of Catherine, as he would only have been aged only 15 at her conception. However Catherine became a member of the new Huntington family in Skelton, though sadly she died at the age of 9 in February 1802.

Ann Huntington was to have a life of tragedy; having lost her father Henry when she was 8, her mother, Ann Hutton died in the June of 1798, less than two months after her marriage to John Huntington. This was to be capped, as we have seen by the loss of daughter Catherine.

Before this loss however, John and Ann had produced their first child, a son, Henry ("Harry"), who was baptised on the 11th January 1799 - just teetering on the bounds of respectability. Another son, John, was baptised on the 12th February, 1802, one day before Catherine was buried. Two years later, on April 22nd 1804, their third son Isaac (the author's great-great-grandfather) was baptised. His future wife, Grace was born to Richard and Mary Hogg in July of the following year. John and Ann completed their family in July 1808, when Margaret was born.

Three other births, germane to the history of the Huntingtons in Skelton, were those of John, in 1810, Thomas 1811, and Joseph, in 1815, to Joseph and Mary Grindal who farmed at nearby Phoenix Hall, just down the road from John and Ann. Apart from the reminder of schooldays at Skelton, we know little about the intervening lives for the next 15 years or so.

The joinery business started by John seems to have prospered, centred as it presumably did , on serving the local farming industry. We have a tithe map of the Skelton area, shewing John's house with its adjoining workshop, and garth, used, one guesses as a small- holding. This is 40-50 yards from the centre of the village, and opposite to where the school has since been re-located. On the opposite side of the road is a house and two or three acres, eventually owned by Isaac and Grace Huntington. Isaac obviously joined his father in his joinery business, and probably Harry did too, for later when he lived down the lane at Riggdyke, he described himself also as a joiner.

The next event noted in the records is an intriguing one: the runaway marriage of Harry on 31st May,1823 to Mary Ann Harrison. This took place,not at Gretna Green, but at Annan, a few miles further over the border of Scotland. Given the circumstances surrounding Harry's parents' young life, it is hard to imagine that they would have opposed the marriage of their 24 year old son, and Mary Ann was 27 at the time of her marriage. Possibly it was done out of a desire for adventure - we shall never know. If so, the adventure was shortlived, for Mary Ann was buried on 26th July 1824, little more than a year after her marriage.

Harry was to marry again, at nearby Heskett-in-the-Forest, on 8th October 1831, this time to Elizabeth Howson, and thereafter until their deaths in 1840, they were to live at Riggdyke, just outside the village of Skelton. Their first child, Ann, was born in June 1832, followed in May 1833, by Grace, and in February 1835, another daughter, Eliza, was born. Finally their son Thomas was born in October 1837. Then tragedy struck; in August 1840, their mother Elizabeth died, aged 38, followed in November of the same year by the death of their father,Harry, aged 41. The first National Census to provide limited personal information was carried out in April 1841, and we see from its records the saddening situation for the children of Harry and Elizabeth. Living in the care of their grandparents, John and Ann Huntington,then respectively 65 and 70 years old were Ann, aged 8 and Thomas, aged 3; living with grandmother Ann Howson, aged 65, was Eliza aged 5, whilst Grace aged 7 was living with her uncle Isaac and Aunt Grace, together with the two sons of Isaac and Grace, cousins John, 5,(the author's great-grandfather) and Joseph, aged 2.

Margaret, the only daughter of John and Ann Huntington had married, John Rothery, described as a mariner, in October 1831, at Cross Canonby, on the west coast. The only record at Skelton is that they returned there in 1832 to baptise their son, Henry Wilson Rothery.

The year 1841 was another bad one at Skelton. On 5th December Isaac died and the close relatives remaining to care for more orphans were becoming scarce. They became scarcer still when John Huntington.died on 20th May 1843,aged 67, and Grace died in November 1847 at the age of 42. Within a few short years all four of the children of Harry and Elizabeth died; firstly Ann,aged 15, in May 1847, Eliza, aged 12, in January 1848, Grace,in July 1850 aged 17 and finally Thomas, at the age of 16, in November 1854.

The 1851 census found Thomas in Wigton, aged 13, described as a Draper's Apprentice, working in the Draper's shop at 10 King Street, for Joseph, the younger of old Joseph Grindal's sons. The same 1851 census at Skelton recorded that Joseph Grindal, aged 77 lived with John Huntington,painter, aged 51,the surviving son of John and Ann Huntington, described as nephew of Joseph Grindal. This he was not in the literal sense, but there is no doubt that the Grindals cared for the unlucky Huntington family.

By now Isaac and Grace's children had also been orphaned; Harry's surviving child, we have seen, was in the care of young Joseph Grindal at Wigton; another orphan, John Huntington, the author's great-grandfather, was recorded in the 1851 census for Penrith, as a Draper's apprentice, aged 14, working for......John Grindal, aged41, described as a Master Draper, employing 4 men. So far it has not been possible to trace what happened in those intervening years to Joseph, the youngest of the orphans. Neither has it been possible so far to trace the widow Ann Huntington. Possibly she took on the care of Joseph, that is if she was still alive. Bearing in mind though, that she would have been 80 at the time of the 1851 census, were she alive then, it is unlikely that she could have undertaken the care of a child. More Likely that she moved nearer to Cross Canonby where her daughter Margaret lived. The most likely custodians of Joseph after his mother Grace's death in 1847, were the Hogg family. Though Richard Hogg had died in 1828, no trace has been found of a death of Mary Hogg, and she would have been about 55 in 1851. Hopefully one day the facts will come to light. Old Joseph Grindal lived on to the grand age of 83, dying in 1857.

We must not leave this chapter in a fog of ignorance, for we know, with hindsight, that young Joseph lived on to be a very successful Farmer, who died at Langwathby, in 1916, at the age of 76, and that his elder brother, John made a career, firstly as a Draper, later describing himself as a Tailor, living in London. More of them later.

Contemplation of all those untimely and early deaths at Skelton leaves one puzzled. No record can be found of any epidemic there; besides, by that time it was customary for the Parish Records to attribute abnormal numbers of deaths if caused by epidemics. We can only speculate that deaths from diseases caused by lack of sanitation, and impure water were rife and regular, especially before the mid-century. Again it is feared that this mystery will remain unsolved.

Probably because their deaths were too sudden to permit the making of wills,none was left by Harry, Isaac or Grace. Their father John Huntington did however leave a will, dated 8th April 1843, (he died 20th May of that year). He appointed his old friend Joseph Grindal, and Joseph's son John, as joint executors. with his wife Ann. He left the whole of his estate to his wife Ann, for her lifetime, and after her decease, on trust, to pay to each of the children of his late son Harry, the sum of ten pounds, upon their reaching the age of twenty one years, (which, sadly not one of them did), in the meantime the interest on those bequests to be applied for their education. He left the sum of five pounds each to the children of his late son Isaac - to John and Joseph, similar provision being made to apply the interest arising, pending their reaching their majorities, to the benefit of their education. To his surviving son, John, and to his daughter, Margaret, he provided that after his widow's death, they should inherit his household furniture.

In material terms, perhaps, not a lot to show for a lifetime of hard work, but he had after all acquired skills, lived in reasonable freedom from want, had been surrounded by good friends in Skelton, and whether by chance or design, had brought his children up in a location where opportunities for education existed, for them and for their children in turn. This latter was a gift not available to all who lived in country villages. Maybe this was a gift to be passed on to later generations, for John Huntington , the son of Isaac, begat a few generations of educationalists and teachers.

A last footnote to the story of the Huntingtons in Skelton, is the record of baptisms in November 1849, and in November 1851, at St.Michaels Church, of Margaret Ranger Wharton, and Elizabeth Wharton, the daughters of Anthony and Mary Wharton, described as a Saddler. Anthony Wharton had married, in January 1824, at Wigton, Mary Huntington, the daughter of Margaret, and the grand- daughter of Mary Huntington,(1757-1840), the youngest daughter of John and Martha Huntington, of Holme Cultram and Wigton. (see chapter six), the ancestor common to all those named in this paragraph. This means that the Wharton children were third cousins, once removed from John and Joseph Huntington. The Wharton family later moved to Temple Sowerby,on the borders of the then Westmorland and Cumberland, where further additions to the family arrived : Hannah Maria, in 1853, Robert William, in 1855, Jane Ann in 1857, and Isabella Ireland Wharton, in 1860. A descendant of Hannah Maria - Mrs Lyn Harpham, living in Tauranga New Zealand, with whom the writer corresponds, kindly sent a colour photograph of a small beautiful tapestry, depicting Joseph and Mary leading the boy Jesus out of Egypt, made by her Great- Grandmother, Mary Wharton (nee Huntington). This has joined other much treasured possessions.

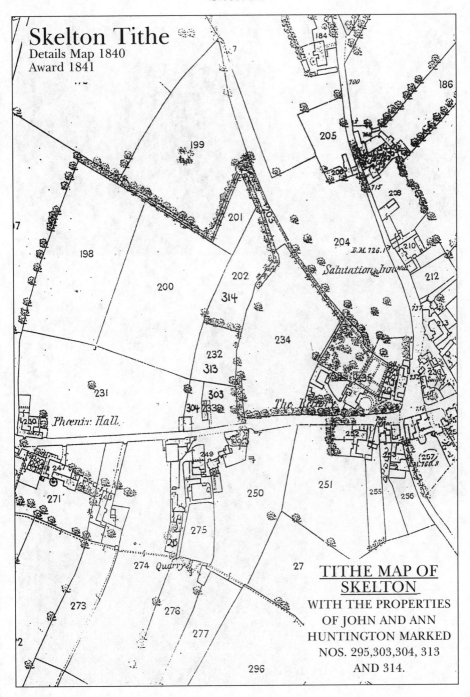

Skelton Tithe
Details Map 1840
Award 1841

**TITHE MAP OF
SKELTON**
WITH THE PROPERTIES
OF JOHN AND ANN
HUNTINGTON MARKED
NOS. 295,303,304, 313
AND 314.

ABOVE: ONCE THE HOME
& JOINERY WORKSHOP IN
SKELTON OF JOHN AND
ANN HUNTINGTON.
TOP LEFT: REAR VIEW
BEFORE REFURBISHMENT
BY THE PRESENT OWNERS

ABOVE: THE ORIGINAL
SCHOOLHOUSE.
RICHT: THE OLD
RECTORY

Skelton

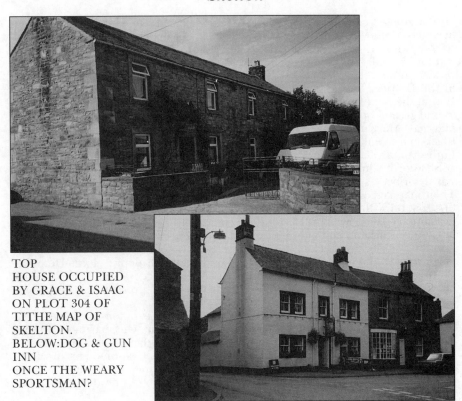

TOP
HOUSE OCCUPIED
BY GRACE & ISAAC
ON PLOT 304 OF
TITHE MAP OF
SKELTON.
BELOW:DOG & GUN
INN
ONCE THE WEARY
SPORTSMAN?

During the period of this story, from the time when Ann Hutton and John Huntington of Sebergham were born, 1771 and 1776 respectively, to about 1850, much had occurred in the outside world : the French Revolution of 1789 had signalled to Europe that a lot of changes were in the offing; followed by the Napoleonic Wars, which not only raised fears of imminent invasion on several occasions, but also created trade problems affecting every part of the country. The period spanned the reigns of four sovereigns, George III, George IV, William IV, and the beginning of the reign of Queen Victoria. At the beginning of that period the bulk of the population lived in the country - in villages like Skelton - but by 1830 half of the population lived in towns thanks to the opportunities created by the Industrial Revolution. The 1840s came to be known as the 'Hungry Forties' as a result of the stagnation of trade, combined with a series of bad harvests. Relief from this stagnation had to await the repeal of the Corn Laws in 1846. Nearer to home the innovation of the railways, starting with the opening in 1825 of the Stockton and Darlington Railway on the east side of the Pennines, signalled a revolution in travel, and this was fulfilled for Cumbrians in 1830 with the inauguration of the Newcastle-Carlisle Railway. For no more would the opportunities of travel, with the widening prospects for jobs and careers, be denied to ordinary people. Along with thousands of others, the

121

Huntingtons would, with comparative ease, be able to seek to make their livelihoods elsewhere in Britain. As we shall see, many of them did just that starting with the last generations born in Skelton.

John, the eldest of the two orphaned sons of Isaac and Grace Huntington, we recall, was next recorded in the 1851 census at Penrith, working as an apprentice in the Drapery business of John Grindal. At that time he was nearly fifteen. Within the next few years he must have crossed over the Pennines, presumably to find greater opportunities in his chosen career. On the 15th February 1863, he married Margaret Ann Turnbull, the daughter of William Turnbull, a Blacksmith, and of Ann Turnbull (nee Smith). They gave their address as Ludworth, a village about 5 miles east of Durham, and the marriage took place at Shadforth Church. Margaret's age was given as 23 and John's as 27, and he was described as a Draper. Margaret had been born at Clarence Row, Stockton. Their marriage was preceded, by about four weeks, by the birth of William, their first son, on 17th January 1863. William, the author's grandfather, was followed in February 1865, by John Henry, They could not have tarried for much longer in County Durham, and although we do not know exactly when they moved to London, we do have a clue, in that there is a photograph of this small family, taken in a studio at Stoke Newington, London, which depicts John Henry at about age eighteen months, and his brother William aged about 3 ½ to 4 years old. So another family had succumbed to the lure of the prosperously beckoning South, and had migrated from its Northern Homeland.

John's younger brother, and fellow orphan, Joseph, is rather harder to trace between the time of his Mother's death, and the occasion of his marriage in 1862. He has not appeared on any of the Census Returns so far studied for 1851. As speculated earlier, he may have been in the care of his Grandmother, or of the Hogg family, but in view of his career as a successful farmer in Westmorland and Cumberland, it is just as likely that he was in the care of one or other of the farming Grindals.

The only milestone in his life available to us is his marriage in May 1862, to Ann Hayton, at Crosby Garrett in Westmorland. They presumably spent much of their early married life in that part of Cumbria, as three of their five children were registered in the East Ward, and baptised at Crosby Garrett. Whether Joseph, in those early days gained some experience in Farming, we do not know; he may have been working for somebody else whilst he learned his 'trade'. In fact, some evidence has been proffered by his grand-daughters that he worked for some time on the railways. This has a ring of truth as the Settle to Carlisle Railway, one of the last to be built, was under construction from 1869 and was completed in 1876, when Joseph was in his early thirties. The line went through Crosby Garrett, where Joseph and Ann lived. The pay would have been attractive for a young man with a growing family. On the other hand, the conditions in which he worked must have been exacting, for the Settle to Carlisle line, like some of those built in Scotland, was carved through hilly country. Most of the workers, or navvies, were itinerant men from out of the immediate locality, many were from Ireland, and lived in very poor, unsanitary circumstances. Joseph, being a local, probably enjoyed better conditions. The settlements and camps on this line were famous, or infamous for their poor standards, and the Sedburgh medical officer for health strongly criticised the one at Dale Head for its overcrowded and cramped state.

Nevertheless it is fairly certain that Joseph regarded this phase of his life on the railway as a transitory one, enabling him to earn high wages for a spell, probably to enable him to save some money towards the day when he and Ann could set up as a farming family.

A subject for speculation has been the question of how, starting from nothing, did Joseph and Ann find the wherewithal with which to acquire the splendid farm at Langwathby Hall which they were able to bequeath to their children, at the end of their lives. The same question arose when contemplating the apparent success of John and Martha Huntington, of Holme Cultram, a century before. In both cases a possible explanation is that both couples may have either inherited, or received help from, the parents of their wives. In the case of John and Martha, the latter's family, the Skeltons were a large and well established one in Allerdale, and, it should be noted that several Huntington generations perpetuated the name of Skelton as a christian name. Likewise the Haytons were well established in Westmorland, and Joseph and Ann's grand-daughters have a belief that they might have helped 'set them up' financially. In both instances, the opportunity having been thus provided, if indeed that is what occurred , had to be well and astutely exploited. Joseph and Ann certainly did that.

Joseph and Ann's first child, Mary Agnes, was born in September 1862, and she married Parker Bowman in 1884, also in Westmorland. So far, little knowledge has been discovered about the Bowman family, but they had a family of five children - Maud Bowman, whom the writer knew in the 1940s at Langwathby, Cumbria; Grace, Edward (Ted), Muriel, and Amy (presumably Amelia). It is believed that Ted had three children by his marriage, the first two of which were named Parker and Eva respectively. Perhaps the publication of this story will bring forth some more information.

The second of Joseph and Ann's children was baptised Elizabeth Ann in September 1864. It is understood that she was referred to as 'Lill'. Elizabeth married John Donald, a widower. It is believed that no children arose from the marriage. A gravestone in Langwathby Churchyard records the deaths of both John Donald and Elizabeth in 1912. George Edward was the next child of Joseph and Ann, and he was baptised at Crosby Garrett in November 1866. George never married, but he and his younger brother Isaac helped run the very fine farm at Langwathby, and in his later years, at least, lived with his younger sister Grace, born in 1969, and baptised in the Methodist Church at Kirkby Stephen. The writer knew well, when he was a junior, not only Maud Bowman, and the kindly Grace, but also the fierce 'Uncle George'. All three lived together in their retirement in a big house overlooking the River Eden, by the bridge at Langwathby.

Special memories are preserved of Grace's pastry, baked each week in a vast oven in the kitchen. Finally came Isaac, in May 1880. When the writer knew these fine folk in the early 1940s, George had retired as a Farmer, running the farm at Langwathby Hall which had been handed on by Joseph and Ann on their deaths in 1916 and 1917 respectively. After the death of Joseph, his farming interests had been left to his two sons, and subsequently George retained Langwathby Hall, and Isaac took on a farm at Millrigg, which sits beside the River Eden, where it is joined by the Crowdundle Beck, between Culgaith and Temple Sowerby. The writer had the privilege, as a junior citizen, to live on this farm for a few months in 1940. Isaac had married Dora Donald, the daughter of Lill's husband, John Donald. Isaac and Dora had two daughters, Margery, born in 1912, and Ann Dorothy (Peggy),born in 1918, both happily still alive, and still

The Solway Plainsmen

living at the family home at Riggside, at Culgaith. Isaac had a fine mixed farm at Culgaith, and was greatly respected in Cumbria. During the war,when he was in his sixties,in addition to farming his 250plus acres, he helped the productivity drive by visiting neighbouring farms in an advisory role.

It has been very difficult to glean more information about Joseph and Ann, which is regrettable, as they led such interesting lives. However, together with the school exercise book from the days of Skelton, my great grandfather must have preserved also a little handwritten note from Joseph to his older brother John :

" I will just give thee my signature to let thee know that I am still alive. Kindest regards to sister."

They had no 'sister', and presumably Joseph was sending his kindest regards to his sister-in-law, Margaret Ann Huntington.

In the course of visiting Langwathby in 1992, the writer bought a booklet, at the village post office, entitled "Langwathby Past and Present" written by a local citizen, Mr. James Christopher Moorhouse, JP., which contained a number of interesting old pictures of the village. This writer wondered whether any of his relatives were among those portrayed. Then, in July 1994, after this chapter had been drafted, there came into his possession a postcard, dated 1912, from the writer's grandfather, William Huntington, then obviously on a holiday visit to Langwathby from London, addressed to his youngest daughter, Doris. The postcard picture is identical to the one on page 44 of Mr. Moorhouse's booklet, picturing a group of men on the banks of the river Eden, just below Langwathby Bridge (which collapsed in 1968), with the caption "Langwathby Sheep Washing". (In his booklet, Mr Moorhouse had explained that the farmers received 1d. per pound more for their wool if they washed the sheep before clipping).The message on the postcard from William Huntington to his daughter was "show this to Auntie (Laura) for she will recognise your grandfather and other relatives." Her grandfather was of course John Huntington, who had also obviously visited Langwathby from London and "the other relatives" were John's brother, Farmer Joseph, and Joseph's sons George and Isaac. John the tailor looks slightly over-dressed amongst his farming companions. One wonders whether, on these visits to Cumberland he ever regretted having exchanged his life in that beautiful setting for the attractions of London.

OPPOSTIE: TOP: LANGWATHBY HALL FARM ACROSS
LANGWATHBY GREEN
CENTRE : THE FARM.
BOTTOM : THE "SIT AND STICK CLUB" IN 1992.

TOP;
LANGWATHBY
BRIDGE .
BOTTOM: THE
SHEPHERDS
INN,
LANGWATHBY

LEFT:
MILLRIGG
FARM OVER-
LOOKED BY
CROSS FELL

CENTRE :
MILLRIGG
FARM
CULGAITH.

LEFT :
TEMPLE
SOWERBY,
ONE OF
CUMBRIA'S
MOST
LOVELY
VILLAGES

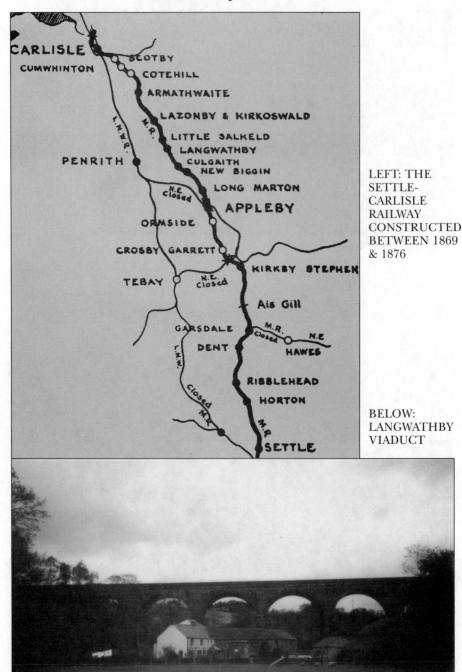

LEFT: THE
SETTLE-
CARLISLE
RAILWAY
CONSTRUCTED
BETWEEN 1869
& 1876

BELOW:
LANGWATHBY
VIADUCT

CHAPTER ELEVEN

CHART NO.16
EXODUS FROM THE PLAINS

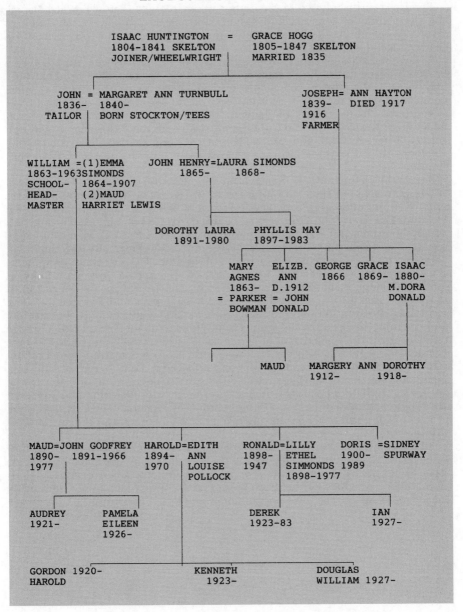

```
                ISAAC HUNTINGTON    =   GRACE HOGG
                1804-1841 SKELTON       1805-1847 SKELTON
                JOINER/WHEELWRIGHT  |   MARRIED 1835


        JOHN = MARGARET ANN TURNBULL          JOSEPH= ANN HAYTON
        1836-  1840-                          1839-   DIED 1917
        TAILOR | BORN STOCKTON/TEES           1916
                                              FARMER


  WILLIAM =(1)EMMA      JOHN HENRY=LAURA SIMONDS
  1863-1963SIMONDS      1865-      1868-
  SCHOOL-  1864-1907
  HEAD-    (2)MAUD
  MASTER   HARRIET LEWIS

                        DOROTHY LAURA    PHYLLIS MAY
                        1891-1980        1897-1983

                        MARY    ELIZB.  GEORGE GRACE ISAAC
                        AGNES    ANN    1866   1869- 1880-
                        1863-   D.1912              M.DORA
                        = PARKER = JOHN             DONALD
                        BOWMAN  DONALD

                                        MAUD    MARGERY ANN DOROTHY
                                                1912-       1918-


  MAUD=JOHN GODFREY  HAROLD=EDITH    RONALD=LILLY     DORIS =SIDNEY
  1890- 1891-1966    1894- ANN       1898-  ETHEL     1900-  SPURWAY
  1977               1970  LOUISE    1947   SIMMONDS  1989
                           POLLOCK          1898-1977

  AUDREY     PAMELA                  DEREK                IAN
  1921-      EILEEN                  1923-83              1927-
             1926-

  GORDON 1920-           KENNETH            DOUGLAS
  HAROLD                 1923-              WILLIAM 1927-
```

This chapter follows the one dealing with the 'Skelton' Huntingtons, and the narrative finished in the mid-nineteenth century, with records from the 1851 census.

The last birth noted on the Skelton family tree was that of Joseph Huntington, in 1839, the younger of the two sons of Isaac and Grace.

The latest births advised to the author were: in 1992, that of Edward Daniel, the third child of Howard and Jacqui Huntington, and in March 1995, of Laurence David, the first child of Graham and Joanne Huntington. Welcome to this wonderful world boys!

In fact the Skelton chapter covered the lives of Joseph, his wife Ann, such as is currently available for their descendants, and likewise of his elder brother, John, and his wife, Margaret. Strangely it is as hard, or harder, to piece together much about the lives of these two, as it has been to do so in respect of much earlier generations. Partly this is to do with the much greater mobility of recent generations. At least with the Cumbrian forbears, all the records lay within that county, whereas John and Margaret started their married lives in County Durham, then shortly afterwards lost themselves in the vastness of Greater London.

Before they left County Durham, John and Margaret produced their family of two boys, William in 1863, and John Henry in 1865. The next clues to their lives are two studio photographs by Edgar Salomon, of 145 Stoke Newington, North London. One is of John Huntington, bearded, dressed in a handsome suit, as a Tailor should be, and looking as earnestly proper as only a Victorian Gentleman could. The other photograph is a little more informative. By the same Mr. Salomon, it portrays the family of John Huntington. He is dressed not quite so elaborately - more workaday; between his knees stands a very apprehensive-looking William, of not more than 4 years of age. In later years William must have hated this picture, dressed as he was in what we would describe as a little girl's dress! Next to John was Margaret Ann, looking a little demure, but solemn, and clutching by his waist the young John Henry - about 2 years old. This age estimate dates the photograph at about 1867, so the family must have become Londoners in 1866/7. Another clue to the time of their migration to London came orally from second cousins Margery and Peggy Huntington, of Culgaith, mentioned in chapter 10. They recalled the story handed down, probably by the author's grandfather (William), their great-uncle, to the effect that Margaret Ann Huntington witnessed the last public execution in England. The Guinness Book of Records dates this event as having taken place on 26th May, 1868, at Newgate Prison, London. The condemned man was one Barrett, convicted of a Fenian bombing outrage, which killed many people. Here is another indicator of how values have, thankfully, changed for it is doubted that many normal people, these days, would regard a public execution as entertainment. The story also reminds us that the 'Irish Question' has been part of life for a very long time, and is by no means merely a 20th century phenomenon.

TOP LEFT: JOHN, MARGARET, WILLIAM & JOHN HENRY HUNTINGTON CIRCA 1866 IN LONDON. ABOVE: MARGARET, CIRCA 1875, AGED ABOUT 35. LEFT: THEIR HOME AT CLAPTON, LONDON. PICTURE SHEWS NO.65 AS NO.67, A SIMILAR HOUSE, WAS DESTROYED IN WORLD WAR 2. THE FAMILY WERE LIVING THERE WHEN WILLIAM & EMMA MARRIED IN 1889

TOP LEFT: WILLIAM BATTING (LEFT -HANDED), JOHN HENRY THE BOWLER

ABOVE: WILLIAM HUNTINGTON, AGED ABOUT 70.

LEFT: EMMA (NEE SIMONDS) CIRCA 1889, ABOUT THE TIME OF HER MARRIAGE, AND AGED ABOUT 25.

ABOVE: EMMA
HUNTINGTON
(NEE SIMONDS)
1864-1907.

TOP
LEFT:LAURA
JANE
HUNTINGTON
(NEE
SIMONDS)1865-?

ABOVE LEFT TO RIGHT: IAN HUNTINGTON, GRANDSON OF WILLIAM
MAUD HUNTINGTON,)SECOND WIFE OF WILLIAM), WILLIAM AT 96,
LILY HUNTINGTON,(NEE SIMMONDS)
MOTHER OF IAN AND WIDOW OF RONALD HUNTINGTON IN FRONT:
HOWARD HUNTINGTON, IAN'S SON. DATED 1959.

ABOVE:THE NORWOOD TECHNICAL INSTITUTE IN SOUTH LONDON, CIRCA 1895 NOW THE SOUTH LONDON COLLEGE, WHERE WILLIAM HUNTINGTON WAS ITS FIRST DIRECTOR, FROM 1895 UNTIL HIS RETIREMENT IN 1923. HIS SON, HAROLD HUNTINGTON, A CHARTERED ACCOUNTANT, ALSO TAUGHT EVENING CLASSES THERE FOR MANY YEARS. WILLIAM HUNTINGTON DREW HIS PENSION FOR FORTY YEARS, UNTIL HE DIED, AGED 100, IN 1963.

During the childhood of the two boys the family seems to have lived in the Hackney/Clapton area of North London, a little to the east of Stoke Newington. A cousin of the author, Ian Huntington, now living in South Island, New Zealand, has preserved a book, entitled "Our Zoological Friends", which was won as second prize, by William Huntington, in 1876, at a Spelling Bee held at the North Bow Congregational Church, - an early sign of his erudition!

Another treasure preserved over the years by Ian Huntington is a photograph, taken in 1974, of William and John Henry playing cricket together, William disclosing that he was a left-handed batsman, and young John Henry looking every inch the determined bowler. The photograph poses a puzzle; the background looks very like Streatham Common, on the south side of London - so very like it that the author believes he could go to the spot from which this picture was taken. But although that location became very familiar to later generations, it was a long way from Hackney and Clapton, even allowing that the whole of Greater London was very generously served with an intricate network of omnibus routes. Maybe William and John Henry were there on an outing, or visiting friends or relatives.

William chose to be a school master, and he had to do it the hard way in order to prosper. He was already pursuing this profession when he married, in 1889, at the age of 26, Emma Maria Simonds, the daughter of a retired butcher from Kentish Town.

The hard way was, after he had married and started a family, to continue to earn his living by teaching, and attending College in his free time, in order to earn a degree. He attended both King's College, of the University of London, (in 1891/2), and also the Queen Mary and Westfield College, (University of London), then called The People's Palace, at Mile End Road, East London. He was awarded a B.Sc. in 1893, at the age of 30. From personal experience in much easier times for travel and study, the author has a modest appreciation of the amount of determination and application which William required to achieve his degree in those circumstances.Almost certainly, Emma provided a great deal of encouragement to aid his purpose.

Meantime Emma Huntington produced their first child, Maud, in 1890, (not in honour of the Maud born 'about 1150'! see chapter one), and was in process of bearing the author's father, Harold, who arrived in 1894.

At this point, William and Emma were living at 58 Darville Road West Hackney. The house still stands, but unfortunately a new and unattractive facade of artificial stone brickwork has been added, though the properties on each side give a good impression of its former appearance. Likewise, No.67 Cricketfield Road, Clapton, the former home of John and Margaret Huntington,(and William and John Henry), appears to have been bombed out of existence during World War 2, and replaced with a 1950s apartment building. Here again, its neighbour, no.65, has survived, and is a good indication of what no.67 was like.

Meantime the wedding bells had rung again for the Simonds and Huntington families; Emma's, younger sister, Laura Jane Simonds, born in 1868, had married, in September 1890, William's younger brother, John Henry. These marriages of two sisters to two brothers, cemented a relationship between the Simonds and Huntington families, which survives to this day, more than 100 years later. This is in spite of distance, because two of Emma and Laura's brothers, elder brother Samuel, and younger brother, Tom emigrated to America. The story is that Sam ran away from home, took ship to America, and that in 1893, his younger brother Tom went there ostensibly to fetch Sam home. They both stayed in the U.S.A., Tom the supposed retriever never to return; Sam coming back to England for a visit in 1912.Both Sam and Tom married and raised families, Tom fathering eight children, three by Ida May, his first wife who died in 1911, and five more by his second wife, Zuma, whom he married in 1913.

Now we must return to the lives of William and Emma Huntington - when we left them they had just produced their second child, Harold.

A new and completely different 'child' came into being in 1895. It was the

TOP LEFT: CHIPSTEAD SURREY 1940 LEFT TO RIGHT: RONALD HUNTINGTON, DEREK, IAN AND LILY.

TOP RIGHT: 1923, ST. LEONARDS CHURCH, STREATHAM; WEDDING OF RONALD HUNTINGTON AND LILY.

LEFT: GORDON HUNTINGTON, SON OF HAROLD AND EDITH HUNTINGTON, THEN AGED 24. HE SERVED IN THE ROYAL CORPS OF SIGNALS FROM 1ST SEPTEMBER 1939, WAS CAPTURED AT TOBRUK, AND ESCAPED FROM ITALY.

Exodus

Norwood Technical Instsitute, in South London. This had been founded in 1859 by Arthur Anderson, (1792-1868), who had been born in the Shetland Islands, at the beginning of the Revolutionary and Napoleonic Wars, and, there being no schooling available, had received his education from his parents. Arthur Anderson, when young, had devoted his time when not washing and curing fish, to self-education. Narrowly avoiding being press-ganged into naval service, he later joined the Navy, in 1808, at the age of 16, seeing service in the Baltic, and off the coasts of Spain and Portugal. Thanks to his efforts at self- education he became a Captain's Clerk, thus learning something of the business management of a ship. In 1815 he was introduced to a Scarborough shipowner, Mr. Christopher Hill, whose daughter he married in 1822. This led him to an introduction to a Mr. Wilcox, just then opening an office as a shipbroker in London, whom he joined. After a long struggle to succeed, the company prospered, and by 1836 Arthur Anderson was a rich man. He settled in Norwood Grove House, where he lived for almost forty years, and in 1859 he built in Norwood a centre of learning and recreation for the poorer inhabitants

After Arthur Anderson's death in 1868, and until 1895, the Institute was controlled by Trustees, and entirely supported by private funds, and local effort. As time went on ,however,the buildings became out of date, and it became increasingly difficult to raise the money necessary for the day to day upkeep. Closure sometimes seemed to be inevitable

However the 1870 Education Act had led to a whole new approach to the question of education; Polytechnics had been opened in and around London, and the local education authorities had begun to provide evening classes in technical and commercial subjects, as well as recreational pursuits. By 1890 the building was hopelessly out of date, so the London County Council was invited to establish a branch Polytechnic in the Institute. Upon their agreement the Trustees offered the Institute to the Technical Education Board of the London County Council. Thus the Institute was saved, and when the building reopened in 1895 as a branch of the Borough Polytechnic, William Huntington was appointed as the Director and Secretary. Three hundred and eight students were enrolled. In 1905 the Governors of the Borough Polytechnic were asked to relinquish the management, and thereafter it came under the direct control of the London County Council, William Huntington being appointed as its first Principal. This post he held until 1923, when he retired, aged 60. The establishment is now the South London College, and celebrates its centenary in 1995.

William Huntington celebrated his centenary in 1963, but we diverge!

In order to live near his new job at Norwood, William and Emma moved house to South London - to 19 Hitherfield Road, about one mile from Streatham Common. Here were born the rest of their brood; Ronald in 1898, and Doris in 1900, whilst, still living over on the north side of London, John Henry and Laura had produced two daughters, Dorothy Laura in 1891, and Phyllis May in 1897.

Tragically, Emma Huntington died, aged only 42, on the 3rd April 1907. Apparently there had been a picnic outing during which she was taken ill with what transpired to be Peritonitis. How stricken must have been the young family, aged from 16 down to 6. The author remembers William Huntington very much as a mellowed old gentleman, but also recalls seeing photographs of him in which he appeared a touch fierce and strict-looking as a Head Master probably felt he should appear in those days. He almost certainly was quite a strict father, and his children must have sorely missed the softening presence of their mother.

It is not known when the family moved to No.94 Lewin Road, at the western end of Streatham Common; it may have been before the death of Emma, and intended to accommodate the growing family. William married Maud Lewis, whom the author remembers as a sweet lady, devoted to him and his, always helping to preserve the fond memories of the departed Emma. They had a long life together, and it was no 'dotage' because until very late in life, William and Maud would go regularly to Old Time Dancing sessions at the Streatham Locarno. The latter establishment organised a party for William and Maud to celebrate his 90th birthday. The place has since been renamed 'The Ritzy Disco'.

William Huntington lived on for about two weeks beyond his 100th birthday, and incredibly he was mentally as well as physically fit (frequently writing letters to the Times, and his M.P.) until his last couple of weeks, when he was admitted to hospital, where he died; the rumour had it that it was because he had not received the Royal Telegram of congratulation!

Having retired in 1923, the forty years for which he received a pension must have been at least as long as the period during which he earned his living.

All seven of his grand-children have memories in common ; of 'Grandfather' with his ever active mind, giving impromptu lessons followed by quizes, whenever they visited him at Lewin Road, or he visited them. He had, despite his alertness, a regular tendency to drop off for a nap, wherever he was, including out in the street! This trait was convenient for his unwilling pupils, for if his testing question was left unanswered for long enough, sleep would come to their rescue. The fond memories are also held for undemanding and kindly Maud, who fell ill shortly before William's admission to hospital, with symptoms which might these days be suspected as those of Ulzheimer's Disease. She died a few years later, in 1965. .

As can be seen from the family tree, William's firstborn,Maud lived to the great age of 87, and like her father, retained her mental and physical alertness for most of her life. Like her father , Maud also was a teacher in a very poor and deprived area of Tooting, until her marriage to John Edward Godfrey, a local government officer, in June 1916.'Jack' had lost a leg shortly after the Great War, as the first world war was then called.

Harold, born in 1894, served as a subaltern in the Great War, married Edith Pollock, became a Chartered Accountant, and succumbed to Parkinson's Disease in 1970, at the age of 75, his wife Edith surviving him by fifteen years, and dying a few days short of her ninety-first birthday.Harold and Edith gave their three sons a very happy childhood, and made sacrifices to give them a good education. These included teaching at evening classes three evenings each week, to supplement an auditor's income. They suffered the continuous anxiety of parents with two sons serving in the Army during World War 2.

William Huntington's youngest son, Ronald, born in 1898, must have falsified his age in his impatience to serve in the Great War of 1914-18, having been only fifteen, rising sixteen when it began, and emerging from it badly gassed. For the rest of his life his lungs, as well as his eyes deteriorated. In spite of this he was a cheerful, often cheeky fellow, definitely the mischief of the family. The last tragedy to strike was his death, in 1947, in a commuter railway crash at Purley,

Surrey.He had married, in 1923, Lilian Ethel Simmonds, at St.Leonard's Church, Streatham. Lily's address was given as No.94 Lewin Road, Streatham, the home of William Huntington, presumably the strict chaperon, whereas Ronald's address was 266 High Road, Streatham, his profession as a Bank Clerk. The witnesses on the marriage certificate included, in addition to William Huntington, "L.Huntington", presumably Laura, Emma's sister, and Herbert H. Pollock, Edith's brother, who had also been blinded by gas in the Great War.

William's youngest, Doris, must also, like Ronald, have been a free spirit. After the Great War she had met an Australian soldier, Sidney Spurway, and in February 1922 she had sailed on the S.S.Osterley for Sidney, one way only, for £120, to marry him. History is silent on the parental attitude to this project, but it is imagined that Stepmother Maud played a sympathetic role. Doris and Sidney enjoyed a happy life, though no children sprang from the marriage. Doris returned only once for a visit to England - in 1931, and the author remembers from the age of only 4, a party at the Strand Palace Hotel, probably a farewell, at which he raised a laugh by handing round somebody's cigarettes to all present; like the Rugby player who kicks a drop-goal he tried to repeat the same trick several times more! Doris outlived Sidney by 16 years, and lived until her ninetieth year, though virtually blind in her final years. Like her father she wrote letters copiously, though her handwriting had the spaciousness of her adopted land.

TOP LEFT LEFT TO RIGHT: 1929 DOUGLAS, KENNETH, AND GORDON HUNTINGTON

TOP RIGHT LEFT TO RIGHT: 1939; EDITH, DOUGLAS AND HAROLD HUNTINGTON AT THE WEDDING OF HILDA POLLOCK (EDITH'S SISTER) TO HENRY VAN DEN BROUCQUE.

LEFT: 94 LEWIN ROAD
STREATHAM, THE HOME OF
WILLIAM
HUNTINGTON.

Here are some recollections of William Huntington by some of his grandchildren:

Ian Huntington, of Amberley,North Canterbury, New Zealand: 'His bristly moustache when he kissed me as a small child; he always brought us educational books on his visits, English for my brother Derek, and Arithmetic for me; he used to come by motor bike, but he took to falling asleep whilst driving, so he gave that up for the train; but then he used to fall asleep in the train, and often missed alighting at our station, having therefore to wait for a return train at the terminus; he would fall asleep in the middle of the family conversation, for a few minutes, and then wake up as bright as a button, and continue where he had left off; when my father (Ronald) was killed, he wrote my mother a practical and lucid exposition on how she should organise her financial affairs - he was then 85! On reflection, as a child I held him in great awe, but there was no doubting that he took a very genuine interest in his grandchildren.'

From Gordon Huntington, now living in Devon: ' I remember taking Grandpa, with my brother Douglas, to the Oval when he was well into his nineties, and he thoroughly enjoyed the day; whilst Freddie Trueman, the fast bowler, was walking back for his run-up, Grandpa fell asleep; when he awoke a few minutes later, Trueman was walking back again, and Grandpa expressed the view that his run-up was rather too long! His last words to me on the night before he died were "You're not such a bad lad, Gordon"

From Audrey Malby, now living in Bournemouth: 'My earliest recollections of Christmas are of those spent very happily at Lewin Road, with Grandfather and Auntie Maud; we used to go there as a family for many years; in 1936/7 I used to go to Lewin Road for "extra coaching" in Maths and French, prior to Matriculation, and I am sure this played a major part in my passing the exams; after the war when my husband Ron started his Chartered Institute of Secretaries course, he used to go to Lewin Road for coaching; I was invited to his 90th birthday party organised by the Streatham Locarno; he was their oldest "Old Tyme Dancer", he seemed to dance the entire evening, and he taught me many old dances of which I had never heard.'

William Huntington's lifetime had spanned the reigns of Victoria, Edward VII, George V, Edward VIII, George VI, and part of Elizabeth II. At its beginning the Union and Confederate armies in North America had fought the Battle of Gettysburg, and at its end,came the Bay of Pigs. In Europe, at its beginning, there had been the Battle of Sadowa, and at its end Europe peered across the Berlin Wall.

William had seen the prosperity and power of British might at its zenith, and witnessed its decline, in relative terms to a more modest role. Railway networks had been developed to boost industrial and commercial prosperity, then to decline in importance, giving way to forms of transport undreamed of in 1863. Communications, which, at the outset of his life had depended on Queen Victoria's penny post,then later upon Gooch's under-sea cable, had become so speedy, that the miracle of listening to Howard Marshall describing, ball by ball, the progress of a Test Match in Australia, was, at his life's end knocked into obsolescence by televised live pictures of Yuri Gagarin in space. Medical science had progressed mightily, to the point at which not only were most known diseases controllable, but new diseases were yet to be invented, such as Aids, Yuppy's Disease, and World Cup Football. From a wonderful character, who had lived through so much great achievement, his final comment on the world was not inappropriate: "You're not such a bad lad, Gordon."

CHAPTER TWELVE

CHART NO.17
THE DESCENDANTS OF ROWLAND &
FRANCES HUNTINGTON OF COCKERMOUTH

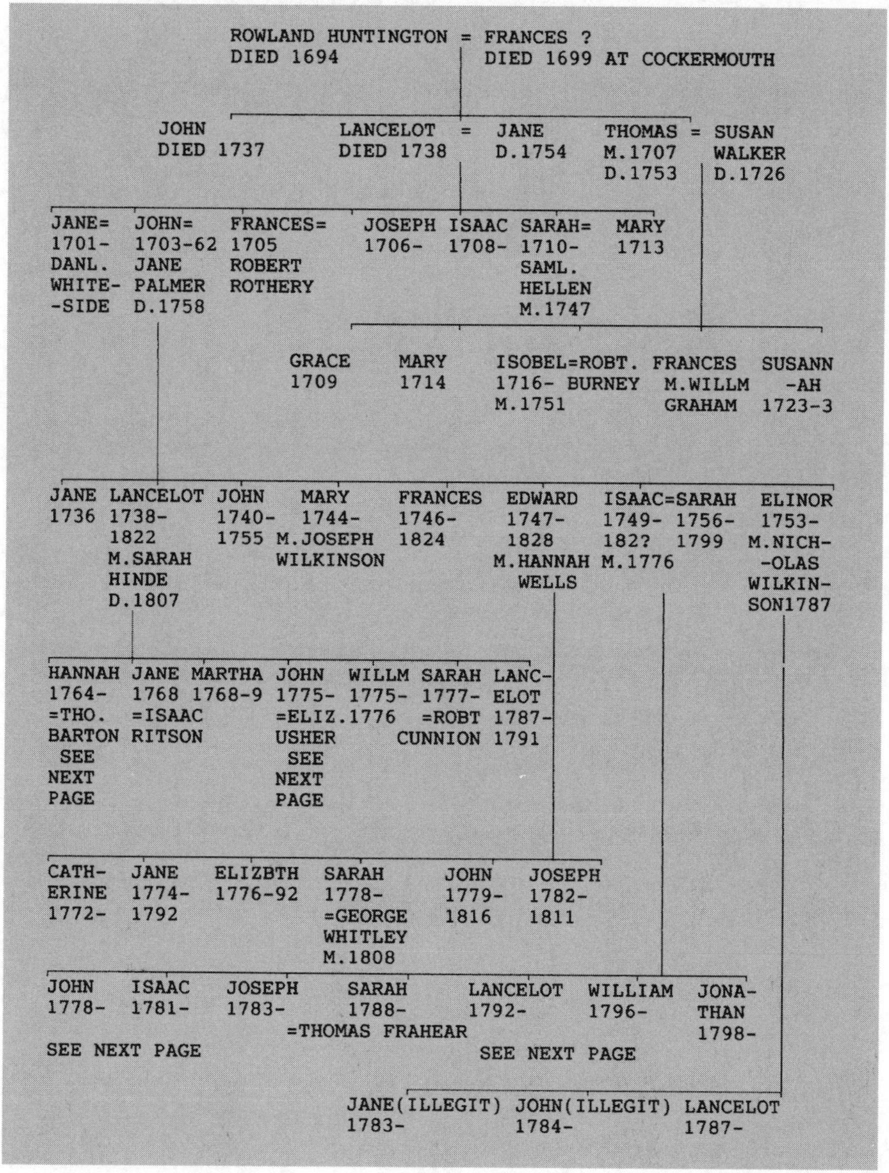

```
                ROWLAND HUNTINGTON = FRANCES ?
                DIED 1694           | DIED 1699 AT COCKERMOUTH


        JOHN            LANCELOT = JANE     THOMAS = SUSAN
        DIED 1737       DIED 1738  D.1754   M.1707   WALKER
                                            D.1753 | D.1726


JANE=   JOHN=    FRANCES=   JOSEPH ISAAC SARAH=  MARY
1701-   1703-62  1705       1706-  1708- 1710-   1713
DANL.   JANE     ROBERT                  SAML.
WHITE-  PALMER   ROTHERY                 HELLEN
-SIDE   D.1758                           M.1747

                    GRACE     MARY     ISOBEL=ROBT. FRANCES  SUSANN
                    1709      1714     1716- BURNEY M.WILLM  -AH
                                       M.1751       GRAHAM   1723-3


JANE LANCELOT JOHN   MARY      FRANCES EDWARD  ISAAC=SARAH  ELINOR
1736 1738-    1740-  1744-     1746-   1747-   1749- 1756-  1753-
     1822     1755   M.JOSEPH  1824    1828    182?  1799   M.NICH-
     M.SARAH         WILKINSON         M.HANNAH M.1776       -OLAS
     HINDE                             WELLS               WILKIN-
     D.1807                                               SON1787


HANNAH JANE MARTHA JOHN   WILLM  SARAH  LANC-
1764-  1768 1768-9 1775-  1775-  1777-  ELOT
=THO.  =ISAAC      =ELIZ.1776    =ROBT. 1787-
BARTON RITSON      USHER         CUNNION 1791
 SEE               SEE
NEXT               NEXT
PAGE               PAGE


CATH-   JANE     ELIZBTH   SARAH    JOHN   JOSEPH
ERINE   1774-    1776-92   1778-    1779-  1782-
1772-   1792               =GEORGE  1816   1811
                          WHITLEY
                          M.1808

JOHN    ISAAC    JOSEPH    SARAH      LANCELOT   WILLIAM  JONA-
1778-   1781-    1783-     1788-      1792-      1796-    THAN
                           =THOMAS FRAHEAR                1798-
SEE NEXT PAGE                        SEE NEXT PAGE

                    JANE(ILLEGIT)  JOHN(ILLEGIT)  LANCELOT
                    1783-          1784-          1787-
```

143

CHART NO.18
FURTHER GENERATIONS OF THE DESCENDANTS OF ROWLAND
AND FRANCES HUNTINGTON OF COCKERMOUTH
CHILDREN OF LANCELOT & SARAH CHILDREN OF ISAAC AND SARAH

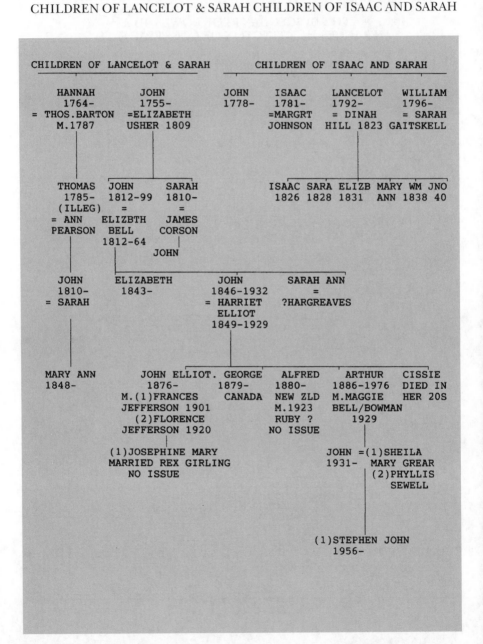

CHILDREN OF LANCELOT & SARAH   CHILDREN OF ISAAC AND SARAH

```
  HANNAH        JOHN        JOHN    ISAAC    LANCELOT   WILLIAM
  1764-         1755-       1778-   1781-    1792-      1796-
= THOS.BARTON  =ELIZABETH          =MARGRT  = DINAH    = SARAH
  M.1787        USHER 1809          JOHNSON HILL 1823  GAITSKELL


  THOMAS    JOHN       SARAH       ISAAC SARA ELIZB MARY WM JNO
  1785-     1812-99    1810-       1826  1828 1831  ANN 1838 40
  (ILLEG)   =          =
= ANN       ELIZBTH    JAMES
  PEARSON   BELL       CORSON
            1812-64      |
                        JOHN

  JOHN       ELIZABETH     JOHN          SARAH ANN
  1810-      1843-         1846-1932     =
= SARAH                  = HARRIET     ?HARGREAVES
                           ELLIOT
                           1849-1929

  MARY ANN     JOHN ELLIOT. GEORGE   ALFRED    ARTHUR      CISSIE
  1848-        1876-        1879-    1880-     1886-1976   DIED IN
               M.(1)FRANCES CANADA   NEW ZLD   M.MAGGIE    HER 20S
               JEFFERSON 1901        M.1923    BELL/BOWMAN
               (2)FLORENCE           RUBY ?    1929
               JEFFERSON 1920        NO ISSUE

               (1)JOSEPHINE MARY               JOHN =(1)SHEILA
               MARRIED REX GIRLING             1931-  MARY GREAR
               NO ISSUE                             (2)PHYLLIS
                                                      SEWELL


                                            (1)STEPHEN JOHN
                                               1956-
```

Cockermouth

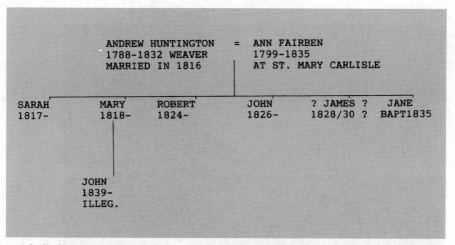

```
        ANDREW HUNTINGTON   =  ANN FAIRBEN
        1788-1832 WEAVER       1799-1835
        MARRIED IN 1816        AT ST. MARY CARLISLE

SARAH       MARY    ROBERT      JOHN      ? JAMES ?    JANE
1817-       1818-   1824-       1826-     1828/30 ?  BAPT1835


        JOHN
        1839-
        ILLEG.
```

Of all the towns in Cumbria, Cockermouth is one of the prettiest and most pleasant. Unfortunately for it there is a rival for the supreme title; the previous county town of Westmorland - Appleby is happily unspoilt, having been made a backwater by its loss of county town status as well as by the motor road which passes by. So the vote for charm has to go to Appleby, whilst Cockermouth deserves the prize for balancing beauty with a certain vivacity.

Claiming Borough status since the thirteenth century, Cockermouth carries its years with grace, and although only a small town, it has about it an air of purposefulness, looking to the future rather than living on its past. Its future and its past largely rest on its key location on the routes from the seaports and industrial towns on the Irish Sea coast, to Carlisle, to Northumberland, to Scotland, and to the south via the Eden Valley or by way of Keswick. Historically it played an important role in the textile industry, and was the home to many people engaged in the manufacture of woollen and cotton goods, linen, hats, and leather products. Its two rivers, the Cocker, and the Derwent, and their tributaries, flowing briskly from the Derwent Fells to the sea, provided the power needed for these industries. Additionally Cockermouth was a natural place to visit for those who sought work, as well as for those who sought to recruit workers, for in addition to its famous annual horse and cattle fair, and regular corn and cattle markets, twice a year it held a Hiring Fair. Here, those seeking work would loiter, waiting for prospective employers of farm or domestic servants to approach them.

Some of the scribes who wrote entries in parish registers were quite informative, often adding the parents' address, or the father's occupation on the baptism register, ages of the parties to a marriage, and again, occupations, even sometimes the names of witnesses. For burials some would give the age of the deceased, and even, rarely, the cause of death. The scribes who made the entries in the registers of All Saints Cockermouth seldom gave more than the basic information required, which is a pity because frequently the registers can be a valuable source of information. It is those additions which help to bring life to our long-gone ancestors

TOP: COCKERMOUTH HIGH STREET
ABOVE : THE CHURCH AT COCKERMOUTH.

LEFT:
LOWESWATER
LOW PARK;
MELLBREAK
FELL IN
BACKGROUND.

RIGHT:
LOWESWATER
CHURCH.

LEFT:
LOW PARK
COMPLEX
WITH VIEW
OVER
CRUMMOCK
WATER.

ABOVE:
HIGH PARK
LOWESWATER

RIGHT:
VIEW
FROM HIGH
PARK OVER
CRUMMOCK
WATER.

So, of the lives of Rowland and Frances Huntington we know nothing except when they died, in 1694 and 1699 respectively, and that they had three sons, John, Lancelot and Thomas.

Of these, only one, Lancelot had a family which perpetuated the family name. For the youngest of these brothers, Thomas described as a yeoman, and his wife Susan, produced a fistful of daughters, Grace, Mary, Isobel, Frances, and Susannah. John, a Waller died in 1730 not having married. Nobly named Lancelot married Jane (name unknown) who presented him with seven children, including three sons, John, Joseph and Isaac.

No more is heard of Joseph and Isaac, the register at this time was very sparse and incomplete, and we must assume that they died in their early years. John Huntington however, a yeoman, married Jane Palmer in 1735, and in their twenty-three years of marriage, before Jane died they had eight children; Jane, Lancelot who was destined to live for eighty-four years, John who died when only fifteen, Mary, who was to marry Joseph Wilkinson, a mariner, Frances, who was to remain a spinster for her long span of 77 years, Edward, who would live until he was eighty-one, Isaac, who as we shall see, lived well into his seventies, and Elinor who was to do her own thing.

John and Jane died within four years of one another, neither of them living long enough to see any of their offspring married. The reader will understand how faceless these folk appear in the absence of any more than the scantiest of information about them; there is no image with which we can visualise them. So we should be thankful when we come across something which throws a little light on their existence, and then is the time to give our imagination rein in the hope that we can conjure up a picture.

John and Jane's eldest son, Lancelot,a weaver, married a lady whose family name was a familiar one in Cumberland - Sarah Hinde, in 1763. They in turn produced seven children, two of whom died in infancy, and one, Lancelot, who died when he was only four. Their eldest, Hannah married Thomas Barton in 1787, having beforehand, in 1785, had an illegitimate son, Thomas. Her sister Jane married Isaac Ritson of Workington in 1797.

Edward, the third son of John and Jane, who as we have seen was to have a long life, married Hannah Wells at Bridekirk in 1771. Whilst waiting for sons they were blessed with four daughters, until finally two sons, John and Joseph arrived. These however died at the ages of 37 and 29 respectively.

Isaac came next in 1749, and he became a weaver. Whereas though, most Cockermouth weavers would trek to the Lorton vale, or wherever their source of wool was to be found and then journey home to Cockermouth to weave it, Isaac took his loom to the wool. He went to beautiful Loweswater, where in 1776, he married Sarah Bell,aged 22 the daughter of farmers John and Sarah Bell, of Latterhead, a hamlet between the villages of Loweswater and Lorton. Sarah had been orphaned when her mother, had given birth to her. Isaac and Sarah first set up home at Low Park, on the lower slopes of Mellbreak, the fell which presides over the northern end of Crummock Water. In all they had ten children, of which three died in infancy, the survivors being John, born in 1778, Isaac, born 1781, Joseph, born 1783, Sarah born 1788,who was to marry Thomas Frahear in 1818, Lancelot in 1792, William, born in 1796, and finally Jonathan in 1798. By 1788, when Sarah was born, the family had moved further up the slopes of Mellbreak to High Park at Loweswater. Both Low Park and High Park are very much still standing, and in occupation, the latter as attractively refurbished holiday apartments, with a magic view over some of the most lovely scenery offered by Lakeland. One can imagine it would have been the perfect location for a weaver's gallery, using the damp air from the lake below.

The birth of Jonathan in 1798 was followed by the tragic death of his mother Sarah, in 1799, and apart from the marriage in 1818 of daughter Sarah to Tom Frahear, witnessed by brother Jonathan, nothing more is recorded of the family in the Loweswater register. It is believed that Jonathan went to Liverpool.

The registers of the surrounding parishes have been searched, but no trace was to be found of this young family comprising a widower Isaac Huntington and six sons. (His only daughter, Sarah, we have accounted for.)His second son Isaac we know, married Margaret Johnson in 1810, at Camerton, but probably they moved out of the county, as there are no subsequent records in Cumberland .

Of Isaac's son Lancelot, we shall hear a little more about his early life later, but in 1823 he married Dinah Hill at Cockermouth, and then the couple moved to Workington, where they were to spend their lives, and produce six children. Likewise William made for Whitehaven, where he married Sarah Gaitskell.

ABOVE:
KIRKSTILE INN AT
LOWESWATER.

LEFT:
GRASMOOR FELL
ABOVE CRUMMOCK

We had lost trace of Isaac Huntington, of Loweswater, after his wife Sarah died in 1799, and it was only by good fortune that further news of him was discovered in a most unlikely way. The sharp-eyed Archivists at Carlisle drew attention to the transcript of a lecture, made in 1891 at Lorton, by one, John Bolton. It was entitled "Lorton as it was eighty years ago". John had lived in that village for a number of years, and he had obviously spent much of his time listening to the recollections of the local senior citizens. Foremost among them must have been his wife's grandmother; at the time of the lecture she was 88 years old, blind, rather deaf, but mentally very sharp, and with an excellent memory. Furthermore her maternal grandfather had been born in 1714, had fought in 1745 against the Scottish rebels at Penrith Fell, and also liked to exercise his excellent memory. So, as John Bolton said in his lecture, his wife's grandmother, drawing on the memories of those two lives, could go back to the early 1700s. Another local with a long memory was 'old Mrs Atkinson'. The lecture must have taken several hours to deliver, or perhaps it was spread over several absorbing sessions. John Bolton himself was an excellent raconteur, and it is plain that he delivered his stories with relish, and in an appropriately local dialect. The whole lecture is very informative about the lives of the folk who had lived in or near Lorton and Loweswater, and by itself represented a social history, very much without tears, giving an insight into ways of life, and ways of entertainment in the days before Radio and Television.

A good instance was his description of the road, on the way from Whinlatter, over the 'new bridge' down to Whit Beck, the road being open (unenclosed) until one came to 'Tenters Fields', the name as he pointed out, giving away the presence of the Woollen industry. The word 'tenters' referred to the tenterhooks on which finished cloth was stretched, and beside this Tenters Field was Lorton Mill, the 'Walk Mill', or Fulling Mill, where the newly woven blankets of wool had to be scoured and cleansed of oil, using Fullers Earth and water. He went on to describe how the 'websters' would come down from Loweswater, bringing their woollens to the tenters, and to the Mill. Each week a cartload of unfinished goods would be brought over Whinlatter Pass, the cart returning to Keswick or onwards, loaded with finished goods. The writer, having worked out ponderously that for websters, read weavers, realised that Isaac Huntington, the weaver, of High Park, Loweswater must have frequented Lorton Mill.

Later on, the lecture descibes some of the buildings in Lorton, and relates yarns about some of the previous villagers. He referred to 'Priest Sewell' (the incumbent from 1821-23, who often officiated at weddings and baptisms at other nearby chapels). "Priest Sewell lived in the house called 'Huntington House' when I was here, (had related Old Mrs Atkinson), that fronts the Cockermouth Road. He owned it, and some fields and farmed them himself..............On his death the property came to the Huntingtons, who were a Loweswater family..............."

And later in the lecture:

"Mr Isaac Huntington lived at High Park, and had a son called Lanty (Lancelot). Isaac was well to do, and had a weaving shop at High Park. It was this family who came into Lorton, and gave the name to Huntington House..................."

So quite a lot was to be learned from this lecture of more than 100 years ago, telling us something about Isaac and his family. He was evidently a successful weaver, who had developed a prosperous local business, and his move to the source of the wool had obviously paid off. Like other weavers in these stories, notably, John Huntington of Abbeytown and Oulton, Isaac had engaged in the weaving business at a period of high demand, and prior to its steady demise, after the introduction of steam looms. Isaac also had that other essential ingredient for success in hand loom weaving; a large supply of offspring. Weaving was very much a family activity, involving quite young members of the family. We do not know how long Isaac lived, but we can assume that he was very much alive and kicking in the 1820s, as he was said to have taken over Priest Sewell's house after he relinquished it in about 1823. At that time Isaac would have been 74 years old. Somehow he comes across as a merry widower.

We now return to Cockermouth, to Elinor, the last offspring of John and Jane Huntington. Elinor gave birth to two illegitimate children, Jane in 1783, and John in 1784, when she was already thirty years old. She married Nicholas Wilkinson in 1787, and after a barely respectable 37 weeks, the Wilkinsons were blessed with a son whom they baptised Lancelot. There is no clue as to the paternity of Jane and John; had Jane been baptised Nicola, or John named Nicholas, we might be able to hazard a guess.

John and Elizabeth (nee Usher), living at Dean, had two children, Sarah born in 1810, and John in 1812. John was a yeoman and married a Lorton girl named Elizabeth Bell. Their first daughter, Elizabeth was baptised at Dean, but we have no record of where their next daughter Sarah Ann and their son John were baptised. John set up a business as a draper in Maryport, and married Harriet Maria Elliot, of Albert Street, Carlisle, the daughter of a China and Glass Merchant. The marriage was solemnized according to the rites of the Wesleyan Methodist Association, at the Carlisle Tabernacle. Five children were born to the marriage; the first being John Elliot Huntington in 1876, the second, George, was born in 1879; Alfred came next in 1880; then Arthur, in 1886, and lastly Cissie, who was to die in her 20s.

The 1881 census for Maryport shews that they lived in 89 High Street, presumably over the shop, that they then had three sons, John E., aged 4, George 2, and Alfred, then aged 5 months,(the other two children yet to be born); that John's father, a retired yeoman, aged 69, was living with them. (Elizabeth, his wife, had died in 1864). John senior died in 1899, aged 87, and in his will he left his estate to his son John, the draper, and a handsome bequest to his daughter, Sarah Ann Hargreaves. (Presumably Elizabeth, his eldest daughter had pre-deceased him). His estate sounded substantial, as he listed 'my customary messuages, and other buildings with the gardens and other conveniences thereto adjoining, also the several closes or parcels of land situate at High Lorton in the parish of Brigham, called Becca High Field, and Becca Low Field, Boon House, Wood, and Becksteads'. It also refers to money, £500 secured on the Maryport Harbour Trust. Clearly he had prospered.

John and Harriet Maria's eldest son, John Elliot, married, in 1901, Frances (Fannie) Jefferson, at the Maryport Wesleyan Chapel. John Elliot was described as a railway clerk, living at 22 Temple Street, Brighton. Frances Jefferson's father, of Maryport, was described as a Master Mariner. Captain Joseph Jefferson was to die, in retirement, in London at the age of 66. He had enjoyed a distinguished maritime career, which had included sailing ships. He had hit the news in 1897 by sailing the four-masted barque, the 'Helensburgh' across the Atlantic, from Hull to New York in twenty days - a record. She later triumphed in a race with two other clipper ships, the 'Glenafton' and the 'Sierra Cadena' from Barry, Glamorgan, to Mauritius, en route to Newcastle, New South Wales. The record for a transatlantic voyage, though, was a clipper, the 'Red Jacket', which in 1854 sailed from New York to Liverpoool in an incredible 12 days. This was, however, from west to east, enjoying more helpful winds and currents.

Extracts from the log of a typical voyage on the 'Helensburgh', this one from Hull, round Cape Horn, and up to San Francisco, in 1900, are fascinating. On this one Nancy Jefferson, Captain Joseph Jefferson's wife kept the log:

July 13th. Sailed from Hull, the tugboat Scotsman towing us 15 miles past the Spurn. We had light variable winds.............

July 20th. The boatswain caught a carrier pigeon on the yard. We are going to make a cage for it...............

Sept 19th. The weather is fearfully cold. saw a small schooner today. Sept

21st Fresh breeze NW with small gain. distance 16 miles

Sept 22nd Fresh breeze from NW. Distance (travelled in 24 hrs.!)5.6 miles. Sept. 23rd Strong gale WbyS under lower topsails very heavy sea, ship labouring heavy at times. This is Sunday, the weather has been something awful... I am glad none of our girls are here..... Sept 25th ... very rough sea longtitude 69.1 W. lat.59.2S. (They were about 200 miles south of Cape Horn.)

The outward log ended ,approaching their destination of San Francisco on November 25th; 135 days after departing from Hull, much of the long voyage involving hardship, to say nothing of the fear and anxiety, whose tenor comes clearly through the words used in the ship's log kept by Nancy Jefferson. Today the journey from Heathrow to San Francisco takes 10 hours! Sailing east to west round Cape Horn, whilst in those days, was no picnic for the faint-hearted, was at least faster, because of the prevailingwinds. The record for the west to east passage, from San Francisco to Liverpool, had been set in 1860/61, by the 'Panama', which completed the voyage in 87 days. As a postscript to the story of the Helensburgh, she was sold in 1906, to a Norwegian company, Rederi A/B, and her name was changed to "Marita". In May 1917, she was posted lost, sunk by a German submarine, in mid-Atlantic.

BELOW: CAPT.& MRS JEFFERSON, & DAUGHTERS, FRANCES (FANNIE) AND FLORENCE MARY, WHO MARRIED JOHN ELLIOT HUNTINGTON IN 1901 & 1920

ABOVE: THE
HELENSBURGH IN
SAN FRANCISCO
HARBOUR.

LEFT TO RIGHT:
JOHN ELLIOTT
HUNTINGTON,
GEORGE, ALFRED
ARTHUR AND
CISSIE
HUNTINGTON

Frances and John Elliot Huntington had just one daughter, Josephine Mary during their all-too-short marriage, 'Fannie' dying in 1919 at the age of 45. John Elliot then married, in 1920, Fannie's younger sister, Florence Mary Jefferson, then aged 34. This marriage took place at the New College Chapel. At this time John Elliot's father, John, had disposed of his drapery business, and was described on his son's marriage certificate as a Registrar of Births, Marriages and Deaths, a post he held at Maryport. No children were born of this marriage.

John and Harriet's second son, George, emigrated to Canada, and remained a bachelor. It is noticeable that many young people, living on the west coast of Cumberland, were very conscious of the beckoning sea, and either migrated or took up a sea-going career. Alfred, the third son of John and Harriet, was just such a one, for he emigrated to New Zealand, where he married a local girl, Ruby, in 1923. There were no children from this marriage. Cissie, the family's youngest, died in her twenties, and her elder brother Arthur has treasured all his life, a letter written by her to him, in January 1915, when he was in Vancouver, British Columbia.

Finally, Arthur, the youngest son, married later than most. He lived in Canada in his young days, working for the Canadian Pacific Railway, and during World War I he joined the U.S. Army, serving in France. After the war he returned to the U.S.A. He eventually returned home to look after his parents, who were ailing. In 1929 Arthur married Maggie Bell/Bowman, whose first husband, a Scots Guardsman, had been killed in France. Maggie Bell was the daughter of a retired farmer. At the time of their marriage, Arthur was 42, and Maggie was 40. There was one son of the marriage - John, born in 1931. Arthur, who lived to the grand age of 90, dying in 1976, served in the Home Guard during World War II.

The current John Huntington, when young, evidently listened to tales of the sea from his aunt Florence Huntington, for she along with the Jefferson family, had sailed many times on Joseph Jefferson's ships. John decided to follow the same career, and became a Master Mariner. In 1955 he married Sheila Mary Grear, and in the next year, their son, Stephen John, was born. Sadly Sheila Mary died, and Stephen John was looked after by Sheila's parents, as John's sea-going commitments made this necesaary. Later John married again, to Phyllis Sewell, and currently, in retirement they are living in the town, which was heaped with laurels at the beginning of this chapter - Appleby.

Hannah's illegitimate son, Thomas moved to Thursby, where in 1809 he married Ann Pearson. They had one son, baptised at Thursby in 1810. John, a yeoman went to Shropshire, where he married a lady called Sarah (surname unknown). They eventually returned to live at Powhill, near the village of Kirkbride, on the Solway Plain. They had one daughter Mary Ann.

John had been described in the 1861 census for Powhill as a landowner and farmer, of 11acres. He died in 1864, leaving Sarah to take out Letters of Administration. Later, in the 1881 census Sarah 79, and Mary Ann 28 and unmarried were described as Annuitants, which signified that they had been left with means of support, and were not, as so many people in those days were, destined to be, paupers at the end of a working life.

One other family which made Cockermouth its home was that of Andrew Huntington, of Carlisle. Whilst in Carlisle he married Ann Fairben, in 1816. He was a weaver, and probably felt that he could succeed more easily in Cockermouth, than in the big city. Andrew and Ann produced five, possibly six children; Sarah in 1817, Mary in 1818, Robert in 1824, John in 1826, possibly a James in 1828/30, and Jane, who was baptised on the 11th January 1835, on which day her mother Ann was buried. Strangely the father Andrew had died in December 1832, so perhaps we should not assume that Ann died giving birth to Jane. Perhaps, on her deathbed she requested that the overlooked baptism of Jane should take place.

A final item on Cockermouth concerns the 1851 census. It includes the Cockermouth Union Workhouse, and the list of inmates made by Mr William

Davidson, Master of the Workhouse, names 110 families, comprising 108 male and 110 female paupers. Prominent among the paupers is the number of Handloom Weavers, thrown out of work by the mechanisation of their tasks. In addition there were a number of old people, ex-sawyers, joiners, labourers, seamen etc., who had evidently had a hard working life, but who became paupers as soon as they were too old to work. It makes sad reading, and in spite of all our current troubles, we can, most of us anyway, today be, as George Bernard Shaw put it, "miserable in greater comfort".

" FAIR BE ALL THY HOPES, AND PROSPEROUS BE THY LIFE"

FANNIE HUNTINGTON, (NEE FRANCES JEFFERSON)
JANUARY 3RD 1902.

CHAPTER THIRTEEN

EPILOGUE

In the course of the research there have been numerous instances of recorded events, which, it has not so far been possible to link accurately, with the narratives of the families set out in the preceding chapters. To a large extent the problem is caused by the hiatus in the recording of events, in the 1640s and 1650s, resulting from the rebellion. The information is related in this chapter in the hope that future research might enlighten us.

CURTHWAITE STRAYS

East and West Curthwaite, although belonging to the parish of Westward, are physically closer to the church at Thursby. Because of this, events, such as baptisms, marriages and burials took place randomly at either church, with occasional use of either Wigton or Dalston churches, further to confuse the researcher.

The family shewn on the tree below obviously belongs to the Westward/Thursby group, as we know that Timothy was sired by one of the Roberts living in the parish. No clue is given to indicate which Robert was Timothy's father. We cannot discover any record of Timothy's burial, nor can we distinguish later marriages or burials of any of his children, except for Jeremiah, who died aged 2.

The only clue which might give us a suspicion about Timothy's branch of origin, lies in the use of christian names, because families did tend to pass these on, usually from parent to child, and sometimes parents would honour their brothers and sisters by naming their offspring after them. The names Timothy and Jeremiah were not frequently used, but it is noticed that the descendants of the 'founder' of the Great Orton branch, Joseph of Thursby, used both of these names for the baptism of children. Possibly therefore, this reflected a close relationship between the families.

CHART NO.20
ROBERT HUNTINGTON

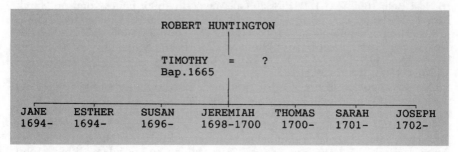

As we have seen in chapter 3 covering Westward/Thursby, and particularly from the speculative tree at the start of that chapter, there was at that time a profusion of Huntingtons in the district, all bursting to generate families (and confusion for future researchers!)

THE PHANTOM GRAFFITISTS OF WETHERAL CAVES

The Wetheral Caves were described as follows by Mr T.H.Hodgson, reporting on a party visit, (C.W.A.A.S. Vol.15, P9 331),

" Little is known of the construction or early history of these caves. They are not mentioned in the register of Wetheral, and it is hardly to be expected that they would be. They are, however, as you see, excavated by the hand of man, being hewn out of the rock, and are clearly not natural caves....... ...here you see a sort of houses dug out of a rock that seem to have been designated for an absconding place..........if not for some hermit to lodge in, being near the monastery.............. there are.....three rooms, each having an independent entrance from the gallery in front............they are generally called St.Constantine's Cells, or by the country people, Wetheral Safeguard..........Dr. Prescott, in his edition of the Register of Wetheral,.. thinks that their position points to their occupation as a place of concealment and safety.............they were....... difficult of access, the only way to come at them being by a steep descent of several yards along a narrow and difficult path. They are approached by a gallery formed by a wall built before the cells, which.............considered to be probably of the fourteenth century............there were three windows and a chimney in it; probably the space between it and the rock was covered by a roof, which would render the cells a tolerably comfortable dwelling. It is likely that these cells may be as old as the time of the Romans, who probably quarried rock here, and that they have subsequently been improved by the monks. There are marks of bolts, which show that the cells had doors.............. .....there is an interesting collection of names and dates inscribed on the rock, and these are given in chronological order " T.Monke, 1573; Oliver Skelton, 1600; W.Byer, 1603; O.S., 1606; Patrick Rv. el,1606; Laine Sibson, 1608; Titus Salkeld, 1606; Oliver Skelton, 1609; Henry Foxcroft,1616; P.E.1616; Robert Briskoe,1617; G.S.1618; R.R.1619; John Salkeld, about 1620; J.T.; S.E., 1631; R.M.1635; Adam Sanderson, 1636; Alexander Maxwell 1639; R.W.,T.W.,1639; T.Hilton 1642; H.G.1651; R.R. 1653; John Dixon, 1650; W.Dixon, 1660; W.Dixon, June 6th 1660; I.N., 1661; Thomas Helme, 1680; John Railton,1670; Roger Carlton (about 1680) G.D.1680; Abraham Dobinson, 1680; John Knight, 1683; John Hunter, 1683; I.P. 1684; Alexander Hodgson, 1686; E.A.1690; George Porter 1692; R.Bell, 1692; T.G.1694; Josiah Gill May 24th 1696; James Tomison,March 14th 1701; Israel Dobinson, March 14th 1701; William Graham, March XXV, 1702; Thomas Sanderson, 1706; G.R.1711 Thomas Wallas,1712; Thomas Morrison, 1716; Joseph Monkhouse,1722; John Simpson, 1724; JOHN HUNTINGTON 1724; T.L. 1728; R.B.1742; J.L.1749; Joseph Harding, 1756; T.Fisher, 1765; R.S.'74;W.M.1786"

This was reported in the "Carlisle Journal" on the 17th July,1868 One has to speculate who these people were; were they indeed fugitives, and if so from whom, and for what reasons? As we have seen, some of them were living in turbulent times, and some at least might have been fugitives from punishment for their religious beliefs, or non-beliefs. Undoubtedly some of the signatories left their inscription for the fun of it; it is intriguing to speculate. Which John Huntington was it who made his contribution to the writing on the wall?

Taking the records of John Huntingtons from the International Genealogical Index, and from Cumberland Parish Registers, for the period, whose names had been ommitted from the I.G.I., there were five possible Johns, of whom one could have been the scribe:

John of Westward, son of Robert and Jane, (1705-1774)
John, son of Thomas and Mary of Thursby (1690-1762)
John, son of Rowland and Frances, of Cockermouth.(Died 1737)
John, son of Lancelot & Jane, of Cockermouth, (1703-62)
John, the Quaker,(Apothecary), of Carlisle, (1691-1747)

It was not likely that it was either of the Johns from Cockermouth, but it could have been any of the others listed above. The odds have to be on John the Quaker; he had more opportunity, living in Carlisle, very close to the site of the caves; he may even have had the necessity to seek shelter there, although, by 1724, Quakers are not thought to have gone in fear of their lives or liberty, and in any case his admission in 1717, as a Freeman of the Carlisle Merchants Guild, indicates his acceptance by the 'establishment'.

CHART NO.21
THE SKELTON CONNECTION

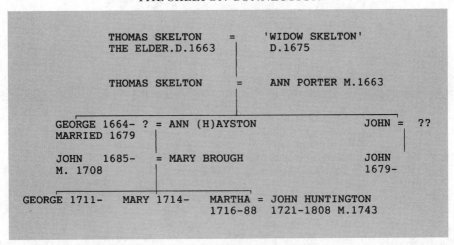

As has been related in the chapter on Holme Cultram, the earliest recorded connection with the Skelton family was the marriage between John Huntington of Thursby and Martha Skelton, in 1743, at what is now called Abbeytown. The word 'recorded' has been used cautiously because there is every likelihood that there may have been earlier links between the families. The Skeltons were a very large and extensive family with branches all over the county. The above tree illustrates the Skelton line down to Martha, and is as far back as we can trace, although other researchers of that family might well be able to track further back.

THOMAS SKELTON - THE ORIGINAL TOM FOOL ?

Lyson's Brittanica, referring to Muncaster Castle, relates that:"In the house are several family pictures, and a curious portrait of Thomas Skelton, 'the fool of Muncaster', who is said to have lived in the family at the time of the civil wars, and of whose sayings there are many traditional stories.

He is dressed in a check gown, blue, yellow, and white; under his arm is an earthen dish with ears; in his right hand a white wand; in his left, a white hat, bound with pink ribbons, and with blue bows, in front a paper on which is written 'Mrs Dorothy Copeland' The following lines are inscribed on the picture:

'The Skelton late fool of Muncaster's last will and testament:"

> "Be it known to ye, oh grave and wise men all That I Thom
> Fool am sheriff of ye Hall,
> I mean the Hall of Huigh, where I command What neither I
> nor you do understand
> My under sheriff is Ralph Wayte you know
> As wise as I am and as witty too
> Of Egremont I have Burrow Serjeant been
> Of Wiggan Bailiff too, as may be seen
> By my white staff of office in my hand
> Being carried straight as the badge of my command
> A low high constable too was once my calling
> Which I enjoyed under King Henry Rawling
> And when the fates a new sheriff send
> I'm under Sheriff prick'd, World without end.
> He who doth question my authority
> May see the seal and patten herely by
> The dish with lugs which I do carry here
> Shews all my living is in good strong beer
> If scurvy lads to me abuses do
> I'll call them scurvy rogues and rascals too
> Fair Dolly Copeland in my cap is placed
> Monstrous fair is she, and as good as all the rest
> Honest Nick Pennington, honest The. Turner both
> Will bury me when I this world go forth
> But let me not be carried o'er the brigg
> Lest falling I in Duggas River ligg
> Nor let my body by old Garnock lye
> But by Will Caddy, for he'll lye quietly
> And when I'm bury'd then my friends may drink
> But each man pay for himself, that's best I think
> This is my will and this I know will be
> Perform'd by them as they have promised me."

Sign'd seal'd and delivered by

Henry Rawling.
Henry Troughton
Th. Turner
Th. Skelton X His mark.

THOMAS SKELTON,(TOM FOOL) THE FOOL OF MUNCASTER.

The Solway Plainsmen

HENRY EDWARDS HUNTINGTON OF AMERICA
NOTE: NO ANCESTRAL CONNECTION IS CLAIMED
IN RESPECT OF THOSE MENTIONED BELOW

The late Henry Edwards Huntington, who died in California in 1927 was the descendant of a line of Huntingtons which could trace its immigration from England back to the earliest times, thought to have been about 1633, and members of the family were founders of settlements and townships which have subsequently become towns and cities.

When he died, Henry left a vast fortune to his widow, Arabella Duval Yarrington Huntington; it amounted to 150 million dollars. In fact Arabella's name by that logic should have been Arabella Duval Yarrington Huntington Huntington, because before she married Henry, and after she had been married to Duval and Yarrington, she had been at first the mistress and later the wife of Henry's uncle, Collis P.Huntington.

It was Collis P. Huntington who had made the huge fortune; starting as a young pedlar in New York, he had achieved a store of his own in up-state New York, before joining the Californian Gold Rush, then acquiring railroad and shipping lines. He became the most powerful of the big four men who controlled the western railroads.

On the death of Collis P Huntington, Henry inherited his fortune, and later married Arabella. Both of them were avid collectors of works of art - books, artifacts, and paintings, especially paintings. They were lavish acquirers of Rembrandts, Vermeers, Reynolds. Their most treasured acquisitions were Gainsborough's 'Blue Boy', and Lawrence's 'Pinkie', the former having been considered priceless, which they acquired from the Duke of Westminster in 1921. It was generally agreed that Arabella had an unerring eye for art, and the Arabella Memorial Collection was housed in the west wing of the Library featuring Renaissance paintings, and eighteenth century French sculpture, tapestries, porcelain, and furniture. Arabella died in 1924, and on Henry's death, the nation was left all their art treasures, and ample funds to house them in a magnificent museum, with its Botanical Gardens, previously Henry and Arabella's home, located at San Marino, in Southern California. Known as "The Huntington", it is one of the American nation's great cultural and educational centres.

Epilogue

WANTED DEAD OR ALIVE - JAMES HUNTINGTON'S DAD

David Huntington, of Carlisle, would very much like this request granted. David wrote that he had plotted his family tree back a few generations, but on the Huntington side, he could get no further than James Huntington, born in 1828, at Cockermouth. He knew that there was a connection with the Skelton family somewhere along the line, and indeed he had plotted that connection as being with his Great-grandfather, John Huntington,(1849-1929). The mysterious James had been that John's father, and he knew that James had been born at Cockermouth circa 1828. Surely enough, the 1881 census for Maryport, Cumberland, records the following:

Rowbrow Top; James Huntington,aged 52, Coal Miner,born Cock'mouth
            Jane"   58   Dearham
            Henry   23   unemployed   "

Main Street   John Huntington   31   Coal Miner   Dearham
                  Agnes   31   "
                  James   8   Scholar
                  Clement   5   "
                  John   5   "
                  Robinson Henry   11months

" So parents James and Jane were living just round the corner from each other, and the Skelton connection was via Agnes, (1850-1929)

A search of the Cockermouth parish register revealed nothing of a baptism of a James Huntington in or around 1828. Possibly the family were 'non-conformist' by religion. It may be that James was a son of Andrew and Ann Huntington, whose tree is shewn in the Cockermouth chapter, and against which a possible James is placed. They were busy producing a family about that time, and they seem to have been rather erratic in their baptismal habits.

Possibly a reader might recognise a connection, and be able to solve this mystery. David Huntington's family tree is given below

CHART NO.22

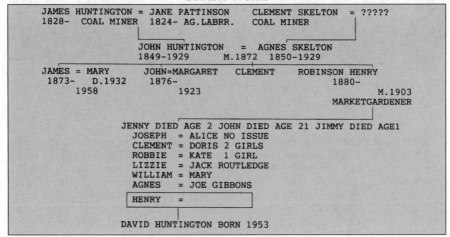

THE CONSTRUCTION OF THE SETTLE TO CARLISLE RAILWAY

As has been remarked elsewhere in this book, the author, born in South London, spent a few months, in 1940, on Millrigg Farm, on the borders of the then Westmorland and Cumberland, travelling the several miles, either by bicycle, or by bus, to attend Penrith Grammar School. Feelings were somewhat ambivalent, as the attractions to a 13 year old boy of the Blitz, preceded by daylight bombing and strafing, (home was very close to Croydon Airport), were exciting to say the least. However his parents already had two sons serving in the Army, and obviously felt they should try to preserve the safety of their youngest!

Compared though with the Surrey suburbs, the beauty of the Eden Valley, where the river provided one of the boundaries to Mill Rigg Farm, overlooked by Cross Fell, and a distant view of the Lake Fells, very easily captured his heart for ever.

ABOVE: THE VIADUCT AT CROSBY GARRETT WHERE JOSEPH AND ANN LIVED DURING THE CONSTRUCTION OF THE RAILWAY

Another of the boundaries to the quite large farm was provided by the Settle to Carlisle Railway, and an everlasting memory is held of the endless trains which passed by more or less round the clock; endless the trains were, both in length, and in frequency, usually laden with munitions and war material. It obviously did not occur to a youngster how grateful the nation should have been for the builders and operators of the line, but it made nevertheless a great impression.

Interest was revived, after a long pause, on discovering the probability that

Epilogue

Joseph Huntington, featured in the chapter on Skelton, had taken part in the building of the railway. During the period of its construction, 1869-1876, he and his family had lived in Crosby Garrett, Smardale, Nateby, and in Kirkby Stephen. As a young man of 30, with ambitions to set up his own farm, the prospect of earning high wages on railway construction, would have seemed heaven-sent. Quite possibly also, by virtue of their locations the opportunity to supplement their income by taking in lodgers from the transient workforce, might have offered another attraction.

Most Cumbrians will have read extensively of the history of building this, most challenging of projects, crossing as it did the high Pennines, and reaching a maximum elevation of nearly 1200 feet. Because of the mountainous terrain, it was necessary to build a total of 19 large viaducts, the largest of which, the Ribblehead Viaduct, involving 24 arches, and stretching 1328 feet, the foundations for the piers reaching down for 25 feet through clay and peat, for the solid rock. Likewise 14 tunnels were needed, the largest at Blea Moor, being over 1_ miles long. In addition scores of road bridges and culverts had to be built, all under severe difficulties, caused by the weather, and by the terrain. The job of getting materials, equipment and men to many inaccessible locations was in itself a daunting one, and for long years, most of the men, often accompanied by their wives and families, had to live in remote and exposed areas, in hutting, or at the very beginning, even in tents. Therefore any workers who could get comfortable lodgings in the homes of such as Joseph Huntington, would have counted themselves very lucky.

The railway was built at the cost of great suffering and hardship, by over 6000 men, and by numerous deaths, from accidents and diseases. The money cost, far in excess of the early estimates, was about £3.6 million.

Certainly the Railway Line repaid the cost and effort handsomely over the ensuing century, after its completion, and happily the attempts to scrap the line have so far been fended off, thanks to a number of far-sighted lobbyists. Long may they prevail!

****

MORE ABOUT THE HUNTINGTONS OF AMERICA

In following up the story, related earlier in this chapter, about Henry Edwards Huntington, it was discovered that he had been a descendant of a line of Huntingtons whose arrival in the New World dated back to 1633 - only ten years or so after the very first migrants from England had settled there; so they really did number amongst the original 'Fathers' of that fledgling nation.

There exists in the U.S.A. a 'Huntington Family Association' comprising over 2000 persons, nearly all of whom have been able to trace their ancestry back to that first family of Huntingtons who landed in New England in 1633. They represent a fascinating story, which is summarised here:

They owe it to Simon Huntington, who was born in Norwich, Norfolk, in England, on August 7 1583, the son of George Huntington, born January 1538, and Anne (nee Fenwick), of Brentford, Middlesex. Simon married Margaret Baret, the daughter of Christopher and Elizabeth Baret, who had been Lord Mayor of London.

Simon and Margaret Huntington sailed from England for America in 1633, on the "Elizabeth Bonaventure", with their four children, William, Christopher,

Simon, and Thomas. The date of William's birth is not known, and it is possible that he may have been a child of Simon Huntington by an earlier wife than Margaret. Likewise the date of Christopher's birth is not known.

Of Simon we do know that he was born in May 1629, and that he was four years old when he landed in America. Although we do not know when Thomas was born, we do know that he was not of age in 1650, and the probability is that he was born in 1632, or 1633.

Simon the emigrant never did land in America, for he was stricken by Smallpox whilst at sea, and his widow, Margaret was left to settle in the new, strange land, with her four young children. Her plight was softened by care and concern provided by the Reverend John Elliot in Roxbury. Then after two years, she married Thomas Stoughton, of Dorchester, and with him shortly moved to Windsor, Connecticut, at the time a new settlement, where she spent the rest of her life. Margaret must have been a very fine woman, not short of courage, and deservedly she married a very fine man, in Thomas Stoughton, who stood very high among the pioneers of the Connecticut settlement.

William, the elder son, did not tarry with Margaret, his Mother, (or Stepmother), and set himself up in Massachusetts, but the other three sons settled in Connecticut, where, though life must have been hard, they prospered and multiplied.

On the following page is shewn a photocopy of the American Declaration of Independence, of July 4, 1776, where in company with the illustrious signatures of Thomas Jefferson, Benjamin Franklin, Robert Paine, and Samuel and John Adams, the reader will find the signature of Samuel Huntington, who lived from 1731 to 1796. Quoting the words of Larry R.Gerlach, in the "Connecticut Congressman: Samuel Huntington", "....(he) is one of those illustrious patriots who formally pledged their ' lives, fortunes and sacred honors' in support of the Revolution, yet are known to modern Americans only as curious historical personages symbolized by quaint signatures on the Declaration of Independence. But unlike many Signers who strode the stage of history briefly during the summer of 1776, and then passed into relative obscurity, Huntington went on to a long and distinguished career in both state and national government. Nonetheless he remains, after 200 years, one of the least- known and most-neglected members of Connecticut's Revolutionary generation."

"Few, if any, men in Connecticut history attained the political prominence enjoyed by Samuel Huntington. Rising from modest origins to become one of the leading lawyers in his native state, he served as an assemblyman, councilor, member of the Council of Safety, assistant judge, and then Chief Justice of the Superior Court, lieutenant governor, and for the last decade of his life, governor. With the exception of two years (1777 and 1782) he annually represented Connecticut in the National Congress from 1776 to 1783; from July 1779 to September 1781, he served as President of the Congress. Ranking sixth in a line of fourteen men who held the Presidency before George Washington, (Samuel) Huntington properly deserves designation as the first official president of the United States, since he was in office when the first federal constitution, the Articles of Confederation, became operative."

However, the honour of recognition as the first President must properly belong to that man of considerable fortitude and courage, George Washington.

As the reader will perceive, we end this story as we started,with Settlers

IN CONGRESS. JULY 4, 1776.

The unanimous Declaration of the thirteen united States of America.

THE SOLWAY PLAINSMEN

BIBLIOGRAPHY

WILLIAM HUTCHINSON :   HISTORY OF CUMBERLAND 1797
BURN/NICOLSON

D. L. W. TOUGH: LAST YEARS OF A FRONTIER.
SANDHILL PRESS

CUMBERLAND ARCHIVES: PERCY SURVEY FOR WESTWARD

CWAAS: CALENDER OF BORDER PAPERS

J. D. MARSHALL &:   THE LAKE COUNTIES FROM 1830

J. K. WALTON   MANCHESTER UNIVERSITY PRESS

J. D. MARSHALL :   PORTRAIT OF CUMBRIA. MAN. UNIV.
PRESS

EDWARD HUGHES :   NORTH COUNTRY LIFE IN THE
18TH.C. VOL2.OXFORD UNIVERSITY
PRESS.

REVEREND C.M.L.BOUCH :   PRELATES & PEOPLE OF THE LAKE
COUNTIES TITUS WILSON & SON
LTD. KENDAL

SUE ALLAN :   GREETINGS FROM WIGTON.
T.MCMECHAN WIGTON

J.L.&.B.HAMMOND :   THE VILLAGE LABOURER.
LONGMAN 1978.

EVE McCLOUGHLIN :   ILLEGITIMACY

ANGUS McLAREN :   HISTORY OF CONTRACEPTION.
PUBLISHED BY BASIL BLACKWELL :
CARLISLE JOURNAL 1869

JACK SIMMONS: THE RAILWAYS OF GT.BRITAIN.
MCMILLAN

K. SMITH: CUMBRIAN VILLAGES

JOHN HATCHER: PLAGUE, POPULATION & THE
ENGLISH ECONOMY 1348-1530.
MCMILLAN 1977.

PETER LASLETT & CO.:   INTRO TO ENGLISH HISTORICAL
DEMOGRAPHY
WEIDENFELD/NICOLSON

PROFESSOR R.W.BRUNSKILL: VERNACULAR ARCHITECTURE OF
LAKE CO.s FABER & FABER 1974

W. ROLLINSON :   LIFE/TRADITION IN THE LAKE DIST.
DENT

C. M. L. BOUCH & JONES :   THE LAKE COUNTIES 1500-1830.
TITUS WILSON

A. B. APPLEBY :   FAMINE IN TUDOR AND STUART
ENGLAND
LIVERPOOL UNIVERSITY PRESS

H. S. BENNETT :   LIFE ON THE ENGLISH MANOR.
CAMBRIDGE UNIVERSITY PRESS 1937

JOHN A. F. THOMSON :   THE TRANSFORMATION OF
MEDIEVAL ENGLANDLONGMAN 1983.

Bibliography

LEONARD COWIE : THE BLACK DEATH AND PEASANTS' REVOLT. WAYLAND 1972

LESLIE CLARKSON : DEATH,DISEASE & FAMINE IN PRE-INDUSTRIAL ENGLAND. GILL/McMILLAN 1975

BARRY REAY : THE QUAKERS & THE ENGLISH REVOLUTION. TEMPLESMITH 1985.

CHANCELLOR FERGUSON : PRESIDENT OF CWAAS. ART. X. THE RETREAT OF THE HIGHLANDERS THROUGH WESTMORLAND IN 1745

MARY HODGSON AND : LYDIA LUNT EXCURSION TO LOWESWATER : A LAKELAND VISIT 1865. MACDONALD & CO. 1987

DAVID R. MacGREGOR : SQUARE RIGGED SAILING SHIPS & CLIPPER SHIPS. ARGUS BOOKS,1977.

DENNIS PHILLIPS : EMPIRE OF LIBERTY U.S.A. HISTORY FROM 1492. PITMAN, 1984

O. S. NOCK : THE SETTLE & CARLISLE RAILWAY. PATRICK STEPHENS, 1992

W. R. MITCHELL & DAVID JOY: SETTLE TO CARLISLE, A RAILWAY OVER THE PENNINES. DALESMAN PUBLISHING

JOHN R. GILLIS: FOR BETTER FOR WORSE; BRITISH MARRIAGES 1600 TO THE PRESENT. OXFORD UNIV PRESS

W. R. MITCHELL : THE LONG DRAG. SETTLE-CARLISLE RAILWAY PUBLISHED BY THE AUTHOR,

FREDK. W. HOUGHTON : & W. HUBERT FOSTER THE STORY OF THE SETTLE-CARLISLE LINE

JOHN PUNSHON : PORTRAIT IN GREY. QUAKER HOME SERVICE 1986

W.R.MITCHELL & N.J.MUSSETT SEVEN YEARS HARD:BUILDING THE S-C RLY. DALESMAN PUBLISHING CO.

JULIET R. V. BARKER : THE BRONTES. WEIDENFELD & NICOLSON

LARRY R. GERLACH : CONNECTICUT CONGRESSMAN : SAMUEL HUNTINGTON, 1731-1796. (THE AMERICAN REVOLUTION BICENTENNIAL COMMISSION OF CONNECTICUT, SERIES XX)

INDEX

Index

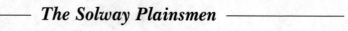

Douglas Huntington